CHOOSING TO LEAD:

The Motivational Factors of Underrepresented Minority Librarians in Higher Education

Edited by Antonia P. Olivas, Ed.D.

Association of College and Research Libraries
A division of the American Library Association
Chicago, Illinois 2017

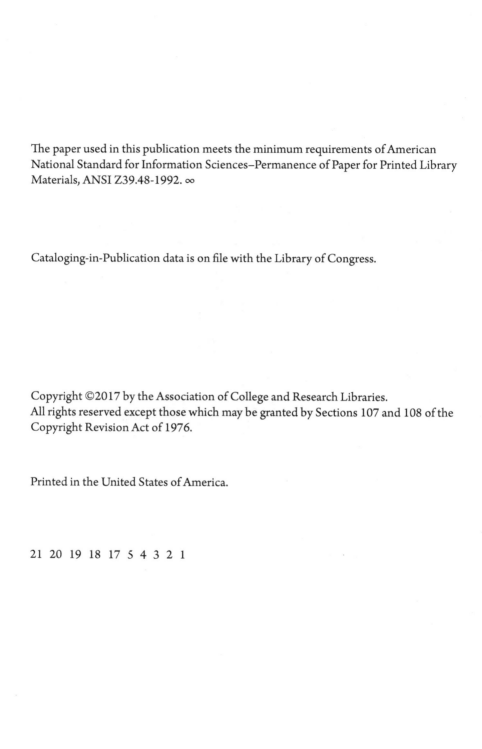

The paper used in this publication meets the minimum requirements of American National Standard for Information Sciences–Permanence of Paper for Printed Library Materials, ANSI Z39.48-1992. ∞

Cataloging-in-Publication data is on file with the Library of Congress.

Printed in the United States of America.

21 20 19 18 17 5 4 3 2 1

CONTENTS

FOREWORD

IN A SEMINAL publication by the Association of Research Libraries (ARL) in 2002, the then university librarian at the University of Illinois at Urbana-Champaign, Paula Kaufman, lamented the fact that research libraries were having tremendous difficulty convincing "frontline librarians" to assume managerial positions and middle managers to take on executive level leadership positions.[1] It is difficult to fathom that the climate has not changed substantively in the last fourteen years and that these problems are not exclusive to the research library community. Anyone who has been tracking the library and information science (LIS) literature with even passing interest must be familiar with the realities and challenges: dramatic transformations in higher education; persistent change, particularly in the area of technology; evolving practices in scholarly communications; relentless budget pressures; generational shifts in the workforce, and attendant (concomitant) workplace expectations and desires for work/life balance; the list goes on and on.

At the International Federation of Library Associations (IFLA) in August 2015, I reported on an analysis that I conducted with the assistance of Sarah McGhee of ARL director placements in the period from 2005 until 2015. In the small sample of 124 research libraries in the United States and Canada that comprise the association membership, 80 percent of institutions had experienced a change in executive leadership (deans, directors, university librarians, principals, etc.).[2] Of course, not all of these positions were filled by professionals previously employed at institutions outside of the ARL membership; a small percentage was filled by sitting ARL directors transitioning to other, in most cases larger, member institutions. An additional data point that is striking from this analysis is related to racial and ethnic diversity of ARL directors. For our analysis, data were culled from the *ARL Annual Salary Survey* over a fifteen-year span, and in it we see an incremental but upward trend in representation of historically underrepresented groups among the director ranks for ARL library directors in the United States.[3] In 2000–01, 4 percent of all ARL directors identified as racial or ethnic minorities, whereas the number was 12.8 percent in 2014–15. For those familiar with the American Library Association's (ALA) *Diversity Counts* reports, these figures align with ethnic and racial representation within the total population of credentialed librarians in higher education (13.9 percent).[4] For the sake of comparison, we distributed a questionnaire to several library directors on campuses of very high or high research institutions per Carnegie classifications. The representation of racial and ethnic minorities in top leadership positions of non-ARL member libraries is quite low—only 6 percent of the total population reporting. Although trends are, generally, more positive in the realm of gender parity, it is also quite astounding to think that at that moment, 43.3 percent of all directors of non-ARL libraries reported having a minimum of thirty-two years of experience in the profession. That number is even more dramatic for ARL directors, who, in the 2013–14 *ARL Annual Salary Survey*, reported having more than thirty-two years of experience for 67.3 percent of the member directors.[5] Certainly one need not explore too much further to find evidence of the much anticipated "graying of the profession." The implications for library leadership—from middle management to executive level—are evident and dramatic.

I begin with these seemingly disparate statistics to illustrate this confluence that is creating a large vacuum, if not a crisis in library leadership. Changing demographics, an evolving workforce, dramatic changes in the higher education and scholarly publishing ecosystems are but a few of the drivers creating this exigency. How are libraries to respond to these trends, to this climate, and ensure that organizations remain relevant to their audiences? What responsibilities do academic libraries (or any other type of libraries) and the academy bear for ensuring that there are reasonable pathways to management and leadership for people from historically underrepresented groups who have few role models and who face systemic, structural barriers to accomplishing that sort of goal? What are the lessons that might be learned from those who have attained positions of leadership, either within libraries, in professional organizations, or in other contexts?

The chapters in this book take a unique approach to the question of leadership and the drivers that motivate one to lead, especially from and for those from diverse racial and ethnic groups too often underrepresented in the LIS profession, and even more in leadership ranks. They offer practical, tactical, and strategic steps that one can take to help explore and realize those goals, but through the lens of positive psychology, that is, with an emphasis on building strengths and fully leveraging one's interests, behaviors, and passions. This is not to imply that the approach ignores or deemphasizes the prevailing challenges that exist for diverse LIS professionals who wish to cultivate leadership skills and pursue those opportunities. However, the perspectives herein provide a narrative that confirms that there are many paths to leadership and many platforms in which to lead, and that one need not have a position of authority to make a difference.

In chapter 2, "Motivate, Lead, Inspire" Oscar Baeza addresses themes that are related to both leadership and management roles and skills in librarianship. The differentiation has plagued theorists, trainers, and practitioners for decades, but if these are discrete skills or behaviors, it is evident from Baeza's narrative that the interplay is common and must be engaged to build credibility and voice in the workplace. The author emphasizes the importance for leaders to be adaptable in their approaches in order to effectively shepherd teams that are diverse in every human dimension and expression. Likewise, he describes his own approach in managing with an emphasis on his direct reports, focusing on creating an environment that ensures their successes in the workplace. This servant-leader approach, although a familiar model, is one that still resonates widely and that has broad applicability, especially in academic librarianship. Still, the importance of self-development and self-care cannot be overstated, especially as it relates to building the confidence needed to lead. Baeza underscores this, as well as the necessity for building intercultural competencies even in ostensibly homogeneous environments.

Many other helpful themes are explored in this chapter, including the importance of involvement in professional organizations and using that engagement as a platform for developing leadership skills; the role of mentoring; and leading when one has no formal title or authority. All of these concepts are important to explore as one develops a personal road map and seeks to realize one's leadership potential.

One of the most interesting things about the LIS profession is the unique stories about how people came to the profession. Finding inspiration from professional role models is commonplace, but so are stories of inspiration from elsewhere, such as family member or friend. Shannon Jones begins and intertwines chapter 3 with personal stories of her journey as an African American woman, a first-generation college student, and an LIS professional with a specific goal. She offers a solid argument for creating a personal leadership vision and for interrogating and changing that vision as one progresses though a career. That vision may be altered as one faces new professional and personal realities or as one sees new opportunity in the landscape. Jones encourages the reader to think about creating a developmental and strategic road map and deploying common planning tools such as short- and long-term goal setting and SWOT analyses, as well as identifying a plan for and dedicating oneself to self-development. As Kouzes and Posner assert, the primary vehicle for the leader is the self, and self-development is leadership development.[6] One cannot overestimate the importance of personal growth and its potential for extending outward to those you are leading.

As with several of the authors in this book, Jones emphasizes the importance of mentorship, but further, of finding appropriate mentors for the context in which you find yourself or to support the specific goals you would like to achieve. In training mentors for ARL programs, I frequently impress upon mentors and protégés or mentees that there is no perfect formula for ensuring that mentoring relationships are rewarding or will even work out. It's by trial and error and by taking time to critically examine expectations and behaviors that strong mentor relationships are built. The idea of self-reflection is one that Jones takes a step further, suggesting that leaders be systematic about taking the time for self-reflection. This may be most critical when things go awry, or when desired outcomes are not met. However, there is tremendous value in reflecting upon successes as well. Leaders must be committed to the process of self-reflection and can become more aware and emotionally intelligent only if they are committed to this practice.

Jones closes her chapter with critical advice about self-care, tying it to effectiveness as a leader and, implicitly, to organizational health. The chapter comes full circle in its emphasis on "self"—that is, understanding that self-development and -care are critical to exemplary leadership. Through her lived strategies, Jones offers a number of pieces of practical advice for aspiring leaders at any level.

By contrast, Michelle Baildon's leadership journey seems less planned, but no less authentic. She begins chapter 4 by providing useful context about the Asian and Asian American experience in the United States, dispelling the myth of the "model minority," at least in terms of their representation in leadership positions in industry, higher education, and other sectors. In what may perhaps be the very cornerstone of this collection of essays, Baildon argues that the characteristics, mind sets, and behaviors that are considered stereotypically "Asian" are the very ones that are interpreted as antithetical to understandings of effective leadership by majority cultures. Institutions like higher education are intrinsically racialized constructs, and, to a great degree, their reward systems are built to advance behavior, language, and processes that are rooted in Western European, heteronormative, male traditions and practices. This can create tremendous challenges for those from these cultures who aspire to leadership roles. Nevertheless, the author recounts her own experience of looking outside of her library organization (initially) to engage and cultivate leadership interests and potential and how those experiences were parlayed into successful campus and library leadership roles.

A prevailing theme across several of these chapters is the importance of self-development, in both informal and formal contexts. Baildon and others cite many positive experiences in leadership development programs, particularly ones geared toward people from underrepresented racial and ethnic groups. Beyond the knowledge, skills, and perspectives that these experiences impart, the potential for expanding one's network and creating community stands out as one of the most significant benefits of these programs.

In this chapter, Baildon reminds us that systemic change takes time and can be, frequently, exhausting and isolating. Nevertheless, remaining true to one's values and remembering that the incremental builds into the aggregate will keep one motivated and authentic in one's leadership journey. The author closes with a compelling case to embrace mindfulness as a practice in our professional lives. The intersection of mindfulness with leadership development has been enormously popular in business literature, especially since the late 2000s. The effect of this practice on emotional intelligence and in other leadership behaviors has been a weighty topic and will continue to evolve in the dynamic, ever-changing, and challenging realm of higher education and of academic libraries.

Two chapters focus on the challenges and rewards of being leaders in the profession from the perspective of being African American women, but through starkly contrasting professional experiences. In chapter 5, Deborah Lilton speaks eloquently about being the first and only African American professional librarian at Vanderbilt University, describing the experience as a "trope of difference." Lilton underscores the importance of learning, through mentorship, about the "unwritten rules" of the organization and how best to manage constant change. She refers to the concept of "cultural taxation," which is the presumed competencies or interests based solely on one's skin color. Many times these cause undue hardship on librarians of color because these presumptions, most often, involve responsibilities beyond their expected duties as well as forcing them to represent voices or populations that they may be unprepared or unwilling to represent.

Lilton offers a unique perspective from one who has professional responsibilities for building collections. She describes her early professional engagement, how it allowed her to think critically about the canon, and how it need not reflect the lived expressions and experiences of only majority cultures.

Where Lilton has spent the entirety of her professional career at one institution, Meredith Evans came into librarianship through a much more circuitous route. In chapter 6, Evans chronicles her journey to archives and libraries via extensive experience in the corporate sector. She describes the interplay between management and leadership skills and how both are necessary to help bring an institution to organizational excellence. She references Steven Covey's 7 *Habits of Highly Effective People* throughout and describes how she developed and applied those habits in her own leadership journey. The inculcation of those behaviors through experiences in the corporate sector, as well through various professional transitions in librarianship, is what helped her reach the professional heights she has achieved. Evans impresses upon her readers that opportunities come from myriad sources and, sometimes, in spite of one's planning. She tells the compelling story of her journey and how remaining a leader in the profession is a matter of principle, but also contingent upon situational factors that motivate her to lead. Evans asserts that her career flourished when she acquired the ability to "balance outside assumptions and personal authenticity."

Hector Escobar's view of the leadership journey is through the lens of an LIS professional from a minority group and the unique challenges that accompany that identification. The author reminds us that leadership is about relationship and that credibility for leaders is often built by genuinely cultivating those relationships and networks. Using his own experience as a framework in chapter 7, Escobar makes the case for why leaders from minority groups are uniquely positioned to manage change and to navigate the choppy waters that often come with leading an organization or unit through transformation. Mirroring John Kotter and the second of his eight steps in leading change, the author emphasizes the need to build "social capital" through networking and relationship building and in the effort to build broader coalitions for the good of the organization.

Certainly, leading change requires the ability to collect, analyze, and interpret data. Escobar walks the reader through the Cycle of Formative Data-Based Decision Making and his personal application of that model to help lead organizational change. Collecting data for data's sake is, perhaps too ubiquitous in the LIS profession. Translating those data into compelling stories that motivate others to act is a true hallmark of an exemplary leader. Escobar concludes his chapter with several valuable pieces of advice for the aspiring leader, especially for those from minority groups.

Jody Gray brings a unique perspective in recounting in chapter 8 her journey as a first-generation college student from American Indian heritage and experience. She emphasizes the importance of building community, or a broad support network, and the importance of those relationships in providing motivation to succeed and lead. Like Escobar, Gray speaks of the need to build "social capital" and the potential benefits this can bring to your career as well as to the institution for which you work. The author builds on Baeza and Jones in her assertions that mentoring— both formal and informal in scope—can provide tremendous benefit to someone from an underrepresented group, particularly as one navigates through the complexities of workplace dynamics and politics. Last, the author highlights how important it is to be deliberate about developing leadership skills. This is particularly complicated for professionals from Native American backgrounds—indeed for all people of color—as it requires one to understand the culture, values, and behaviors of one's identity groups, but also those of the majority cultures upon which the system of rewards and success is built and from which leaders typically emerge.

Chapter 9 focuses on Le's public service and the skills that can be developed from undertaking leadership roles in numerous contexts: library, campus, community, and in professional organizations in local, regional, national, and international forums. The author accepted or actively pursued leadership positions in numerous instances, but was highly selective about the roles undertaken based on his comfort level with the amount of responsibility for the assignment. Le accepted progressively more responsibility as his experience and confidence grew. The author impresses upon the reader that it is critical to seek out employment opportunities with organizations that support and reward public service engagement for LIS professionals.

This collection of essays offers considerably more than an academic look at leadership development strategies. The stories offered here provide authentic and personal views, from highly diverse perspectives, about why one might pursue management or leadership positions in LIS, the challenges that people from historically underrepresented racial and ethnic minority groups face when they attempt to enter that landscape, and practical strategies for developing oneself to ensure success. Further, the authors take a holistic approach to the topic, challenging the reader to consider how issues of self-development, self-reflection, and self-care should be intrinsic to this process. A deep understanding of how our multiple identities connect and must be nurtured will allow us to reach our full potential as leaders in the workplace, in the profession, and beyond.

—Mark A. Puente
*Director of diversity and leadership programs at the
Association of Research Libraries (ARL)*

NOTES

1.   Paula Kaufman, "Where Do the Next 'We' Come From? Recruiting, Retaining, and Developing Our Successors," *ARL: A Bimonthly Report on Research Library Issues and Actions from ARL, CNI, and SPARC,* no. 221 (April 2002): 1–5.

2. Mark A. Puente and Sarah McGhee, "Change at the Top: ARL Director Trends, 2005–2015" (poster presentation, 81st annual conference, International Federation of Library Associations and Institutions, Cape Town, South Africa, August 15–21, 2015).
3. Canadian members of the association do not report racial or ethnic demographics for their institutions.
4. Denise M. Davis and Tracie D. Hall, *Diversity Counts* (Chicago: American Library Association, 2006, rev. 2007); American Library Association, "Diversity Counts 2012 Tables," A-5, p 2. http://www.ala.org/offices/sites/ala.org.offices/files/content/diversity/diversitycounts/diversitycountstables2012.pdf.
    Note that the *Diversity Counts* tables have an additional classification ("Two or more races") not included in the *ARL Annual Salary Survey*.
5. Martha Kyrillidou and Karen Wetzel, *ARL Annual Salary Survey 2000–2001* (Washington, DC: Association of Research Libraries, 2001); Martha Kyrillidou and Shaneka Morris, ARL Annual Salary Survey 2013–2014 (Washington, DC: Association of Research Libraries, 2014).
6. James M. Kouzes and Barry Z. Posner, The Five Practices of Exemplary Leadership (San Francisco, CA: Jossey-Bass, 2007).

BIBLIOGRAPHY

American Library Association. "Diversity Counts 2012 Tables." http://www.ala.org/offices/sites/ala.org.offices/files/content/diversity/diversitycounts/diversitycountstables2012.pdf.

Davis, Denise M., and Tracie D. Hall. *Diversity Counts*. Chicago: American Library Association, 2006, rev. 2007.

Kaufman, Paula T. "Where Do the Next 'We' Come From? Recruiting, Retaining, and Developing Our Successors." *ARL: A Bimonthly Report on Research Library Issues and Actions from ARL, CNI, and SPARC*, no. 221 (April 2002): 1–5.

Kouzes, James, and Barry Z. Posner, *The Five Practices of Exemplary Leadership*. San Francisco, Jossey-Bass, 2007.

Kyrillidou, Martha, and Shaneka Morris. *ARL Annual Salary Survey 2013–2014*. Washington, DC: Association of Research Libraries, 2014.

Kyrillidou, Martha and Karen Wetzel. *ARL Annual Salary Survey 2000–2001*. Washington, DC: Association of Research Libraries, 2001.

Puente, Mark, and Sarah McGhee. "Change at the Top: ARL Director Trends, 2005–2015." Poster presentation, 81st annual conference, International Federation of Library Associations and Institutions, Cape Town, South Africa, August 15–21, 2015.

ACKNOWLEDGMENTS

TRADITIONAL ACKNOWLEDGMENT SECTIONS begin with the author thanking family, close friends, and possibly their own higher power. Since this is my first book, I am not going to stray far from tradition. My first acknowledgment of gratitude indeed goes to God. Without my faith and His guidance, I don't think I personally would have had the motivation to pursue this topic any further and look for my own reasons for staying and wanting to lead in this profession. As predicted, I want to next thank my family for being supportive and excited about this project. I know you all *still* don't fully understand what I do, but I know you're proud of your "Dr. Little Sister Toni" anyway. Virginia, Ramon, Bongo, and the rest of my dear familia: You have all kept me grounded and never let me forget where I come from.

Next, I would like to thank all of the authors in this book who shared their personal stories of motivation. For some of you I know this writing project was a labor of love and for others I know it became an intense act of labor! However, you persevered and helped me produce this important and inspirational story to share with our community. We can all be proud of this book because I feel it shows glimpses of our weakest moments but highlights our strengths and explains why we stay in this profession. I know for some of you writing your chapters opened some painful wounds, but I hope those experiences help motivate you to pursue other research opportunities that dig deeper into some of the issues you shared in this book. Unintentional (or even intentional) acts of racism, microaggression, disrespect, and insult that create hostile work environments are an undeniable part of some of our professional journeys, but I hope this writing experience helps you to seek counteractive measures to those injustices by focusing on what keeps you getting up in the morning and going to work in a profession where many of you may be "the only one." Thank you again for your hard work and your willingness to share your experiences and expertise. It is my hope that your stories will inspire others to take a positive psychological approach when researching underrepresented minority librarians. It is my deeper hope that your stories will encourage other librarians of color to look at their own motivational factors and also seek leadership positions in academic libraries themselves.

I would like to also thank my dissertation committee for planting the seed for this book. Dr. Carolyn Hoffstetter saw that my research proposal had the potential to be something bigger than what I could tackle in a dissertation and inspired me to take my ideas to a larger platform. I feel this is the start of something greater than even one book…

Additionally, I would like to thank the editors, book designers and illustrators, and publishers at ACRL. Starting this book proposal with Kathryn Deiss and the blind peer-review committee who approved its creation, and ending with Erin Nevius who confidently (and competently) took over the reins to see this project to completion, I especially want to thank them for their guidance and their patience as deadlines came and went! Thank you for not giving up on this project.

Finally, I want to personally thank you, the readers. I hope the stories and advice within these pages inspire you to consider your own motivations and take appropriate actions that will help retain and advance underrepresented minority academic librarian leadership.

Chapter 1

INTRODUCTION

Antonia P. Olivas

THE INSPIRATION FOR this book came from my own dissertation writing experience and my own leadership journey. I remember standing in front of my dissertation committee defending my proposal to look at the retention factors of African American, Latin@, American Indian, Asian Pacific Islander, and Chinese American academic librarians. My goal was to cover all the American Library Association (ALA) caucuses and find out why librarians like me, people from underrepresented minority backgrounds, were defying the odds and staying in a profession that was basically chewing us up and spitting us out (or so it felt). I originally thought I was going to write my dissertation on the virtues of mentoring relationships and how that could help increase retention and promotion efforts, but my committee reined me in and told me to focus on two of the populations instead of all of them and to really look at the literature and focus on the gaps of library leadership retention and promotion efforts. At first, I felt deflated. I wanted to change the library world for all librarians of color! How dare these academics hold me back? It wasn't until my chair said, "Toni, you're not writing a book here. You need to finish in a reasonable amount of time. This is a project you can think of *after* you've finished your dissertation." So, I swallowed my pride and focused on African American and Latin@ academic librarians and vowed to return to my original goal later.

I devoured library literature focusing on retention and promotion of minority academic librarians and found it depressing. Very little seemed to be working, and most of the literature focused on reasons why under-represented minority librarians were leaving the profession. After thirteen years of being a librarian, I realized that I had become part of a very limited club. So I asked myself, "If things are so bad in librarianship for librarians of color, and if the literature is correct and we are losing the diversity fight in libraries, why are some of us *staying*?" That's when I identified the gap in the literature I wanted to focus on—the successes of library retention and promotion! Luckily I happened to find the dissertation entitled "Toward a Theory of Individual Differences and Leadership: Understanding the Motivation to Lead."[1] Upon further investigation, I found that Dr. Chan wrote other works with Drasgow and Rounds based on motivation to lead theory.[2] I finished my dissertation on the motivation to lead of African American and Latin@ academic librarians and soon after embarked on this adventure of getting back to my original goal: include the motivation to lead of more underrepresented minority librarians. This time, however, instead of interviewing participants, I wanted people to speak for themselves. Their only parameters for writing each chapter asked them to briefly discuss the hardships they encountered on their paths to library leadership but to focus on the main reasons they *stayed* in the profession. I asked them to delve deeper and look at their own motivations to lead and to share with the readers some advice and words of wisdom for their own paths.

Like the authors in this book and the many librarians of color who continue to work in the profession (or have unfortunately left the profession), I faced some pretty negative and sometimes unbelievable things on my library leadership journey. Microaggressions, bullying, questioning of my "librarian validity" (because obviously I must have acquired a job based on mandated diversity quotients and not because I was qualified), and blatant exclusion from important meetings or projects are just a sampling of what I and others like me (including some of the authors in this book) experienced, or continue to experience. Yet there is something intrinsic that keeps me going, keeps me motivated to want to stay and lead in this profession. For me it's the overwhelming sense of obligation and my love of teaching and learning. There are so few Latin@ librarians in academia, and there is a growing number of Latin@ college students, so I feel I need to be visible and present to help those students succeed. Many of the authors in this book have similar reasons, but others have their own valid and fascinating reasons.

WHY DOES A PERSON CHOOSE TO LEAD?

The real question is: why does a person choose to lead in an environment where she or he is traditionally labeled "the minority"? Over the years many library researchers found that underrepresented minority librarians leave the profession for various reasons: microaggressions, discrimination, burnout, and lack of opportunity, to name a few,[3] but what motivates some of these academic librarians to *stay* in the profession and, more importantly, what motivates them to *want to lead*? Many of the stories in the following pages will show that some of these individuals stay (and eventually lead) out of a strong sense of obligation, a sense of pride, and the sheer enjoyment of leading others.

Historically and statistically speaking, the image of a white female librarian sitting behind a reference desk is not too far from the current reality.[4] Not surprisingly, academic libraries are most often led by white women,[5] while the percentage of underrepresented minority academic librarians in managerial or leadership positions is staggeringly low. To put it more bluntly, eight out of 112 Association of Research Libraries (ARL) library deans belong to one of four non-Caucasian categories, namely American Indian/Native Alaskan, Hispanic, black, or Asian/Pacific Islander.[6] These numbers are fairly similar in proportion to the greater college and university settings. In fact, 78 percent of US college and university administrators are from white backgrounds, while only 22 percent are from underrepresented minority or "unknown" backgrounds.[7]

Why are these demographics not changing to match the US population? The Environmental Systems Research Institute (ESRI) and the US Census Bureau reported a significant increase of ethnic and racial diversity within the United States between 2000 and 2010.[8] These organizations go on to say that in fewer than twenty-five years, minorities will likely be the majority in the country. Although these numbers show a steady increase in the underrepresented minority population, leadership numbers in the academic world, especially academic libraries, do not reflect the same growth pattern. Why is this important?

The National Center for Education Statistics (NCES) reported a steady increase of underrepresented minority students entering colleges and universities nationwide.[9] As more underrepresented minority students graduate from high school and seek postsecondary opportunities, the numbers of underrepresented minority educators, especially library leaders, will need to keep up in order to help these students succeed.[10] This is significant because diversity in libraries, especially library leadership, is an important factor when developing library policies and services for students. It is also significant because library leaders are also responsible for creating welcoming, safe learning environments for all students, including underrepresented minority students.[11]

College and university libraries are generally at the forefront of change in higher education and have the power to provide diverse educational environments that prepare students to succeed in diverse societies,[12] yet studies suggest that educational institutions in the United States continue to perpetuate existing social inequalities by modeling their settings to benefit mainly white students and their families.[13] Regardless of good intentions and self-perceptions of being open and welcoming to all students, as many academic libraries self-identify, a majority of white librarian presence in colleges and universities presents a limited range of ethnic role models for students. In addition, a majority of white librarian leaders also limits the variety of role models for underrepresented librarians to follow.

Once again the question is asked, why aren't more underrepresented minority academic librarians in leadership positions? There are several factors, such as high recruitment efforts but low retention and promotion efforts, microaggressions, discrimination, and a lack of understanding of what actually motivates an underrepresented minority librarian to want to become a leader in the first place. The chapters in this book will look at just that. While the authors briefly discuss some of the challenges they faced while in the profession, they also take a positive inquiry approach in their essays and focus more on their strategies for becoming the leaders they are today. They talk about the internal and external motivational factors that drove them into taking leadership positions, not just in their libraries but also within their universities and the profession as a whole. Many of the authors "lead from the middle" and discuss how they effect positive change at their institutions without formal leadership titles.

This book examines factors behind the underrepresented minority academic library leadership achievement gap and explores the motivation to lead of current underrepresented minority academic librarians. Each chapter takes a personal examination of the author's leadership journey and delves into the individual's motivation to lead in academic libraries. Suggestions on how to pursue leadership roles are also shared. This book is the first of its kind to delve into the motivational factors of underrepresented minority academic library leaders, and it is the editor's hope to see more studies and stories that focus on our successes in the profession. By learning about what actually works in retention and promotion of some, perhaps the profession can build on what these library leaders have done to help retain and promote current and aspiring library leaders.

THEORETICAL FRAMEWORK

While the authors in this book discuss their motivations to lead and offer suggestions to help aspiring underrepresented minority library leaders, much of what they discuss is founded on actual quantitative and qualitative research. Both internal and external motivations are important to leadership development, yet psychology of leadership can be difficult to understand. Leader motivation is an important factor to investigate in greater detail, especially within a profession where more underrepresented minority leaders are needed.

MOTIVATION TO LEAD

Most of us are familiar with Maslow's, "Theory of Human Motivation,"[14] which includes the five essential human necessities: physiological, safety, belonging, esteem, and self-actualization. According to Maslow's theory, if these basic human needs are not met, a person will potentially suffer both physical and mental harm. However, the theory also stated that once a person meets all of these needs, that person is equipped to accomplish his or her full potential. Chan and Drasgow built on this by adding other factors that contribute to their own groundbreaking theory.[15] Motivation to Lead (MTL) theory looks at influences contributing to a person's *desire* to lead based on four major factors: personality traits, values, leadership self-efficacy, and previous leadership experiences. Not surprisingly these factors are different for each person, with a variety of combinations that ultimately affect his or her desires, or motivations to lead. Based on several other motivational theories, including, but not limited to, Fishbein and Ajzen's Theory of Reasoned Action and Triandis's Theory of Interpersonal Behavior,[16] Chan and Drasgow felt these theories provided a framework for understanding the psychological nature of a person's motivation to lead as well as discovering the dominant factors in a person's wish to lead. Based on these factors, Chan and Drasgow developed three dimensions of motivation identity: Affective Identity, Social Normative Identity, and Non-calculative Identity.

Affective Identity suggests that a person is motivated to lead others by an innate desire that comes from the satisfaction and pleasure of simply being a leader. Many of the authors in this book definitely fit this description. They speak of how much they thoroughly enjoy leading others and see themselves as natural leaders. According to Chan and Drasgow, these individuals tend to be charismatic, outgoing, and very sociable. People who score high in Affective Identity value competition and achievement, and they tend to have more previous leadership experience than their peers. These individuals tend to be more confident in their own leadership abilities and actively seek out opportunities to display their leadership abilities.[17]

Social Normative Identity suggests that a person is motivated to lead by feelings of commitment or obligation to a group or norms that are prevalent in certain social environments. Individuals who score high on the Social Normative scale have a strong sense of social obligation to others, are accepting of social hierarchies, and reject social inequality. These leaders tend to have substantial past leadership experience and confidence in their leadership abilities. Some of the authors in this book discuss feelings of "being the only one" and having a sense of obligation to either "pay back" others who have helped them achieve their status or to "pay it forward" and set an example for others like them.

Finally, Non-calculative Identity suggests that motivation can be viewed as a running scale. The more calculative a person's motivation to lead, the more likely it is that person will aspire to lead in order to enjoy the benefits related to the position. The less calculative the individual's motivation to lead, the more likely it is that person will *not* look at the costs and benefits related to the leadership role. Most, if not all, of the authors in this book certainly took calculative steps in deciding whether or not to lead in their organizations.

SIGNIFICANCE OF THIS BOOK

Diversity in the workplace is certainly a challenge for nearly every organization, but diversity in leadership positions is an even greater challenge, especially in academic library settings. As mentioned before, there is very little research on what motivates underrepresented minority librarians to stay and actively seek leadership positions. It is important to understand these motivations in order to help more underrepresented minority academic librarian pursue a position in library leadership. I hope that once we get the conversation started on how to identify and nurture motivations of these valuable populations, current library leaders can better help increase diversity in academic librarianship. This book provides feedback on underrepresented minority retention issues in academic libraries. It provides information on the perceptions of diversity retention and promotion issues by underrepresented academic librarians, and it gives current academic library leaders a greater understanding of how to most effectively nurture and promote underrepresented minority librarians into positions of leadership. Ultimately current academic library leaders have the responsibility for making sure successful change regarding retention and promotion of underrepresented minority librarians takes place. We hope the individual voices in this book will help inspire the reader to begin looking at what is actually working in regard to retention and promotion efforts.

NOTES

1. Kim-Yin Chan, "Toward a Theory of Individual Differences and Leadership: Understanding the Motivation to Lead" (PhD diss., University of Illinois at Urbana-Champaign, 1999), http://hdl.handle.net/2142/82262.
2. Kim-Yin Chan and Fritz Drasgow, "Toward a Theory of Individual Differences and Leadership: Understanding the Motivation to Lead," *Journal of Applied Psychology* 86, no. 3 (June 2001): 481–95, http://dx.doi.org/10.1037/0021–9010.86.3 .481; Kim-Yin Chan, James Rounds, and Fritz Drasgow, "The Relation between Vocational Interests and the Motivation to Lead," *Journal of Vocational Behavior* 57, no. 2 (September 2000): 226–45, doi:10.1006/jvbe.1999.1728.
3. Jaena Alabi and Pambanisha Whaley, "Recruiting and Retaining a Diverse Faculty Body: The Role of Microaggressions and Incivility" (slides for presentation, 2nd annual ALAHEDO Comprehensive Diversity Conference, Auburn, AL, October 31, 2013), https://aurora.auburn.edu/bitstream/handle/11200/44673/ Recruiting and Retaining_final.pdf?sequence=1; Denise M. Davis and Tracie

D. Hall, *Diversity Counts* (Chicago: American Library Association, 2006, rev. 2007), http://www.ala.org/offices/sites/ala.org.offices/files/content/diversity/ diversitycounts/diversitycounts_rev0.pdf; Joseph R. Diaz, Jennalyn Tellman, and DeEtta Jones, *Affirmative Action in ARL Libraries: SPEC Flyer 230* (Washington, DC: Association of Research Libraries, June 1998), http://old.arl.org/bm ~doc/spec-230-flyer.pdf; Sharon K Epps. "African American Women Leaders in Academic Research Libraries," *portal: Libraries and the Academy* 8, no. 3 (July 2008): 255–72, doi:10.1353/pla.0.0001; Tracie D. Hall, "Race and Place: How Unequal Access Perpetuates Exclusion," *American Libraries* 38, no. 2 (2007): 30–33; Mark D. Winston, "Diversity: The Research and the Lack of Progress," *New Library World* 109, no. 3 (2008): 130–49, http://dx.doi.org/10.1108/ 03074800810857595.

4.   American Library Association, "ALA Demographic Studies," March 2012, http:// www.ala.org/research/sites/ala.org.research/files/content/March%202012%20 report.pdf.

5.   Martha Kyrillidou and Shaneka Morris, *ARL Annual Salary Survey 2014–2015* (Washington, DC: Association of Research Libraries, 2015), http://publications .arl.org/ARL-Annual-Salary-Survey-2014–2015/.

6.   Ibid.

7.   Thomas D. Snyder and Sally A. Dillow, "Table 287: Employees in Degree-Granting Institutions, by Race/Ethnicity, Sex, Employment Status, Control and Level of Institution, and Primary Occupation: Fall 2011," in *Digest of Education Statistics, 2012,* NCES 2014015 (Washington, DC: National Center for Education Statistics, December 2013), 415, https://nces.ed.gov/programs/digest/d12/tables/ dt12_287.asp.

8.   Esri, *Minority Population Growth—The New Boom: An Analysis of America's Changing Demographics* (Redlands, CA: Esri, 2012), http://www.esri.com/library/ brochures/pdfs/minority-population-growth.pdf2012; United States Census Bureau, "Most Children Younger Than Age 1 Are Minorities, Census Bureau Reports," news release, May 17, 2012, http://www.census.gov/newsroom/releases/ archives/population/cb12–90.html.

9.   Thomas D. Snyder and Sally A. Dillow, "Table 302.50: Percentage of 18- to 24-Year-Olds Enrolled in Degree-Granting Institutions, by Level of Institution and Sex and Race/Ethnicity of Student: 1967 through 2012," in *Digest of Education Statistics 2013,* NCES 2015–011 (Washington, DC: National Center for Education Statistics, May 2015), 395, http://nces.ed.gov/programs/digest/d13/tables/ dt13_302.60.asp.

10.   Thomas D. Snyder and Sally A. Dillow, "Table 315.60: Full-Time and Part-Time Faculty and Instructional Staff in Degree-Granting Postsecondary Institutions, by Race/Ethnicity, Sex, and Selected Characteristics: Fall 2003," in *Digest of Education Statistics 2013,* NCES 2015–011 (Washington, DC: National Center for Education Statistics, May 2015), 509–10, http://nces.ed.gov/pubs2015/2015011 .pdf.

11.   Hall, "Race and Place."

12. Mark D. Winston, "The Importance of Leadership Diversity: The Relationship between Diversity and Organizational Success in the Academic Environment," *College and Research Libraries* 62, no. 6 (November 2001): 517–26, http://crl.acrl.org/content/62/6/517.full.pdf+html.
13. Pierre Bourdieu and Jean-Claude Passeron, *Reproduction in Education, Society and Culture*, 2nd ed. (Thousand Oaks, CA: Sage, 1990); Jenny Gordon and Gretchen Generett, "Introduction to Special Issue: Social Justice and Education," *Journal of Educational Foundations* 25, no. 1–2 (Spring 2011), Factiva (ED-FOUN0020110429e71100001); Jeong-Hee Kim and Kay A. Taylor, "Rethinking Alternative Education to Break the Cycle of Educational Inequality and Inequity," *Journal of Educational Research* 101, no. 4 (2008): 207–19, EBSCOhost Academic Search Premier, http://dx.doi.org/10.3200/JOER.101.4.207-219; Annette Lareau and Erin McNamara Horvat, "Moments of Social Inclusion and Exclusion: Race, Class, and Cultural Capital in Family-School Relationships," *Sociology of Education* 72, no. 1 (January 1999): 37–53, doi:10.2307/2673185.
14. Abraham H. Maslow, "A Theory of Human Motivation," *Psychological Review* 50, no. 4 (July 1943): 370–96, EBSCOhost PsycARTICLES, BF1.P7.
15. Chan and Drasgow, "Toward a Theory of Individual Differences."
16. Martin Fishbein and Icek Ajzen, *Belief, Attitude, Intention and Behavior* (Reading, MA: Addison-Wesley, 1975); Harry C. Triandis, *Interpersonal Behavior* (Salt Lake City, UT: Brooks/Cole Publishing, 1977).
17. Chan, Rounds, and Drasgow, "The Relation between Vocational Interests."

BIBLIOGRAPHY

Alabi, Jaena, and Pambanisha Whaley. "Recruiting and Retaining a Diverse Faculty Body: The Role of Microaggressions and Incivility." Slides for presentation, 2nd annual ALAHEDO Comprehensive Diversity Conference, Auburn, AL, October 31, 2013. https://aurora.auburn.edu/bitstream/handle/11200/44673/Recruiting and Retaining_final.pdf?sequence=1.

American Library Association. "ALA Demographic Studies." March 2012. http://www.ala.org/research/sites/ala.org.research/files/content/March%202012%20report.pdf.

Bourdieu, Pierre, and Jean-Claude Passeron. *Reproduction in Education, Society and Culture*, 2nd ed. Thousand Oaks, CA: Sage, 1990.

Chan, Kim-Yin. "Toward a Theory of Individual Differences and Leadership: Understanding the Motivation to Lead." PhD diss., University of Illinois at Urbana-Champaign, 1999. http://hdl.handle.net/2142/82262.

Chan, Kim-Yin, and Fritz Drasgow. "Toward a Theory of Individual Differences and Leadership: Understanding the Motivation to Lead." *Journal of Applied Psychology* 86, no. 3 (June 2001): 481–95. https://www.researchgate.net/publication/11920242_Toward_a_Theory_of_Individual_Differences_and_Leadership.

Chan, Kim-Yin, James Rounds, and Fritz Drasgow. "The Relation between Vocational Interests and the Motivation to Lead." *Journal of Vocational Behavior* 57, no. 2 (September 2000): 226–45. https://www.researchgate.net/publication/222519302_The_Relation_between_Vocational_Interests_and_the_Motivation_to_Lead.

Davis, Denise M., and Tracie D. Hall. *Diversity Counts*. Chicago: American Library Association, 2006, rev. 2007. http://www.ala.org/offices/sites/ala.org.offices/files/content/diversity/diversitycounts/diversitycounts_rev0.pdf.

Diaz, Joseph R., Jennalyn Tellman, and DeEtta Jones. *Affirmative Action in ARL Libraries: SPEC Flyer 230*. Washington, DC: Association of Research Libraries, June 1998. http://old.arl.org/bm~doc/spec-230-flyer.pdf.

Esri. *Minority Population Growth—The New Boom: An Analysis of America's Changing Demographics*. Redlands, CA: Esri, 2012. http://www.esri.com/library/brochures/pdfs/minority-population-growth.pdf2012.

Epps, Sharon, K. "African American Women Leaders in Academic Research Libraries." *portal: Libraries and the Academy* 8, no. 3 (July 2008): 255–72. doi:10.1353/pla.0.0001.

Fishbein, Martin, and Icek Ajzen. *Belief, Attitude, Intention and Behavior: An Introduction to Theory and Research*. Reading, MA: Addison-Wesley, 1975.

Gordon, Jenny, and Gretchen Generett. "Introduction to Special Issue: Social Justice and Education." *Journal of Educational Foundations* 25, no. 1–2 (Spring 2011). Factiva (EDFOUN0020110429e71100001).

Hall, Tracie D. "Race and Place: How Unequal Access Perpetuates Exclusion." *American Libraries* 38, no. 2 (2007): 30–33.

Kim, Jeong-Hee, and Kay A. Taylor. "Rethinking Alternative Education to Break the Cycle of Educational Inequality and Inequity." *Journal of Educational Research* 101, no. 4 (2008): 207–19. EBSCOhost Academic Search Premier, http://dx.doi.org/10.3200/JOER.101.4.207-219.

Kyrillidou, Martha, and Shaneka Morris. *ARL Annual Salary Survey 2014–2015*. Washington, DC: Association of Research Libraries, 2015. http://publications.arl.org/ARL-Annual-Salary-Survey-2014-2015/.

Lareau, Annette, and Erin McNamara Horvat. "Moments of Social Inclusion and Exclusion: Race, Class, and Cultural Capital in Family-School Relationships." *Sociology of Education* 72, no. 1 (January 1999): 37–53. http://www.jstor.org/stable/2673185.

Maslow, Abraham H. "A Theory of Human Motivation." *Psychological Review* 50, no. 4 (July 1943): 370–96. EBSCOhost PsycARTICLES, BF1.P7.

Snyder, Thomas D., and Sally A. Dillow. "Table 287: Employees in Degree-Granting Institutions, by Race/Ethnicity, Sex, Employment Status, Control and Level of Institution, and Primary Occupation: Fall 2011." In *Digest of Education Statistics, 2012*, NCES 2014015, 415. Washington, DC: National Center for Education Statistics, December 2013. https://nces.ed.gov/programs/digest/d12/tables/dt12_287.asp.

————. "Table 302.60: Percentage of 18- to 24-Year-Olds Enrolled in Degree-Granting Institutions, by Level of Institution and Sex and Race/Ethnicity of Student: 1967 through 2012." In *Digest of Education Statistics 2013*, NCES 2015–011, 395. Washington, DC: National Center for Education Statistics, May 2015. http://nces.ed.gov/programs/digest/d13/tables/dt13_302.60.asp.

————. "Table 315.60: Full-Time and Part-Time Faculty and Instructional Staff in Degree-Granting Postsecondary Institutions, by Race/Ethnicity, Sex, and Selected Characteristics: Fall 2003." In *Digest of Education Statistics 2013*, NCES 2015–011, 509–10. Washington, DC: National Center for Education Statistics, May 2015. http://nces.ed.gov/pubs2015/2015011.pdf.

Triandis, Harry C. *Interpersonal Behavior*. Salt Lake City, UT: Brooks/Cole Publishing, 1977.

United States Census Bureau. "Most Children Younger Than Age 1 Are Minorities, Census Bureau Reports." News release, May 17, 2012. http://www.census.gov/newsroom/releases/archives/population/cb12-90.html.

Winston, Mark D. "Diversity: The Research and the Lack of Progress." *New Library World* 109, no. 3 (2008): 130–49. doi:10.1108/03074800810857595.

————. "The Importance of Leadership Diversity: The Relationship between Diversity and Organizational Success in the Academic Environment." *College and Research Libraries* 62, no.6 (November 2001): 517–26. http://crl.acrl.org/content/62/6/517.full.pdf+html.

Chapter 2

MOTIVATE, LEAD, INSPIRE

Oscar Baeza

ACCORDING TO MY ten-year-old daughter, to get to a leadership position, you have to be smart, responsible, brave, and fair. Listening to her reminded me of the importance of the inner child we all have. Things are much simpler when you are ten years old, and as I try to find a good set of words to define leadership, I realize she is pretty much on target. In order for a person to be a leader, they* have to possess some knowledge of what they are doing. They must also be responsible and demonstrate their ability to lead. A person seeking a leadership position must also demonstrate bravery; it takes a lot of courage to take on leadership positions. A leader must be fair and be able to manage situations and conflicts as well. I commend my daughter's efforts to find the proper words for defining leadership, but it takes more than just a couple of words to explain fully the process many of us go through to land a leadership position. I am sure there are countless opinions, definitions, and theories about the course humans have taken to become leaders, managers, presidents, and so on. But I ask myself whether or not there exists a correct path toward that one key position many of us desire? Does a philosophy exist on the correct path toward a "crown-ship"? I believe not; it is our experiences, educa-

---

* In this chapter, the singular *they* is used as a gender-neutral pronoun.

13

tional backgrounds, upbringing, and own personal views that define leadership and set our path of attaining it. This chapter is not about the correct way to achieve a management position. Instead, the following pages offer a glimpse of a personal reflection of my journey and advice on what I believe works to achieve leadership status as an underrepresented minority academic librarian. In addition, I provide information backed by research on various topics and subject matters on leadership. In no way am I an expert in the subject of librarian leadership; however, my fifteen-plus years in the profession and the research I have conducted on leadership give me a useful perspective on the topic.

INTRODUCTION

My mother taught me a very important lesson growing up; she once said to me that as a Mexican American, I would have to work two times harder than whites just to be able to compete here in the United States. Twenty-five years later, I realize that I am still working twice as hard. I ask myself, "How have we failed to move beyond racism and discrimination as a society and as a country?"—not to mention that many people of color grow up in difficult situations like poverty. According to the Pew Research Center, the two largest minority groups, Latin@ and African Americans, have had the highest percentage of people living in poverty within the last fifty years.[1] Is this not the land of opportunities, and do we not have a black president in the White House? The march on Washington led by Martin Luther King Jr. took place over fifty years ago, and yet we are still having the same conversation about the inequalities that exist here in America. Our prisons continue to overflow with people of color, and more recently, it seems Latin@s have been the target of deportation. The echoes of discrimination, racism, and stereotypes reach far and affect every part of our lives. I believe many educational institutions, businesses, or social establishments feel, or at one point or another have felt, the damaging effects of racism and the lack of diversity. General Electric was sued in 2013 by an African American woman who claimed she had to withstand a hostile and racist work environment.[2] Donald Trump's insensitive comments, in his quest for the Republican 2016 presidential nomination, about Mexican immigrants have hurt several of his business ties: Macy's, NBC, and NASCAR are just some of the companies that have separated from the tycoon.[3] Academic libraries are not strangers to this manifestation. A study conducted in 2006 at Portland State University Library stated that many of the students of color surveyed felt that the library should have a more diverse staff.[4] The lack of diversity in the profession I have grown to love drives a devastating dagger of complexity in trying to understand its falls. Nevertheless, the library profession has been able to overcome some hard historical disasters, and today it still lingers high above the clouds of success. The lack of diversity in library leadership positions still begs for answers and even questions.

MY JOURNEY

My professional journey began fifteen years ago, and since then I have learned a thing or two about what it takes to succeed. My first professional position was as a supervisor, and my official title was Public Services Supervisor (PSS) for the Mission del Paso Library at El Paso Community College. I was twenty-four years old and had limited experience in a supervisory role. Nevertheless, I was ready and took charge of the department, and for eight years I led my library team. My eight-year stint taught me many things about management. One of the first things I learned was the term *adaptable*. The ability to adapt in the workplace is common in today's workforce. Employers expect their employees to be able to work as a team and also independently.[5] A former supervisor of mine gave me my first piece of advice as I ventured into this new position. I recall her counsel about people and their mood swings. A good leader must be adaptable to those he or she is leading. People have different personalities, some are introverts, others are extroverts, and some, well, we just don't know exactly what to label them, but they exist. Extroverts tend to be those individuals who are filled with energy and express it very well. Introverts are also filled with energy, but they tend to seek solitude and prefer to be quiet. Carl Jung defined extroverts as those who grab energy from others, while introverts are those who gain energy from aloneness.[6] Working with and managing extroverts and introverts was not easy, but having general background information on these personality types was helpful. However, the most important tip on adaptability is having an understanding of who you are as an individual. My undergraduate psychology professor once told us that the most important thing to know at an undergraduate level of study in psychology is yourself.

In my journey, I also learned about the importance of understanding culture. According to speaker and author on diversity Sondra Thiederman, understanding and having knowledge of your own culture is important to understanding other people's values, upbringing, and way of life.[7] Granted, in a city that is over 80 percent Latin@, the majority of my employees were of Latin@ heritage; nevertheless, they were all different. Each one of them had their own story to share and a journey to talk about. So just the fact that they were all of Latin@ descent did not automatically mean they were all the same. Appreciating people's diverse backgrounds, regardless of their skin color, religion, or political views, is important to being a successful leader. Take the time to know your employees or the team you are leading. Many will argue that it is dangerous to become too friendly with the staff you're managing; however, I tend to believe that if they get to know you and you mean well, then they will work hard for you.

Titles in the workplace are important. However, titles mean nothing if the people you're managing don't believe in you. In my continuous journey as a supervisor, my loyalty was not to the department head or the dean, but to the people I was leading. A former dean of mine once taught me that his main responsibility was to his employees and not his employer. His main job was to make sure that his staff had all the resources necessary to do the job and, in essence, he worked for his employees. The notion that we work for a certain employer was embedded in me a long time ago. Therefore, as a supervisor, I had to change my way of thinking and begin putting this belief into practice. One of the first things I did after learning about this notion was to make sure my staff was happy and comfortable in their positions at work, in addition to being knowledgeable about what they were doing. Constant communication, group meetings, and trainings were just a few of the initiatives that I quickly implemented. I have always believed that people will work hard if they know what they are doing and are happy doing the task. I am also a big believer in bringing out the best in people by using the theory of emotional intelligence. Emotional intelligence is having an awareness of yourself and those around you and making the best working situation out of both. Adrian Schoo stated that it is also about "priming positive attitudes and behaviors."[8] Many athletic coaches use this concept by placing people in certain positions on the sports field that they know those athletes will excel in. You have to have an eye for this sort of practice, but most important, you have to be patient and listen to detail. Practicing positive leadership skills, where a leader builds and infuses healthy relationships through teamwork, recognizing staff abilities, and creating a healthy environment, is an excellent model to follow in any leadership position.[9] Another way is to simply ask your employees what they like to do. I did the same thing by getting to know my team and then simply asking them what they liked to do, and in the process, I paid attention to detail. One of my employees was a website guru and had background training in webpage development. I quickly had him assisting and teaching me and others about webpage development. Another employee was really creative, so she took charge of library displays, marketing and advertising events and activities. Challenging your team members and giving them projects based on what they like and are good at is an excellent way to get the best out of your employees.

Another very important observation I made in my journey as a supervisor was the importance of trusting your employees and believing in them. Building trust in a relationship will strengthen the partnership and create a better work environment. Charles E. Watson wrote that trust within an organization, whether it be from subordinates to management or vice versa, will help strengthen the team concept, which leads to better business or organization production.[10] My immediate supervisor believed in me, and when people believe in you, you start believing in yourself. I never thought I would actually reach the ranks of faculty at a college, much less have the title *Librarian* next to my name. But I eventually entered graduate school, and I have to thank my boss at that time for never doubting me. This trust from my supervisor allowed me to also trust and believe in my subordinates, which eventually led them to trust and believe in me.

After my eight-year experience as a Public Services Supervisor, I received my master's in library science and was given an opportunity to become an academic librarian at El Paso Community College Valle Verde Library (EPCC). Faculty librarians at EPCC are instructors, and most of our time is spent working with students, either at the reference desk, in a classroom, or on a one-to-one base. Librarians are also required to join college committees and be a part of the college's organizational and leadership team. The PSS job was a staff position that supervised the personnel who worked in the circulation department. The position also oversaw the library and maintained its upkeep. Public Services Supervisors work under the direction of a faculty head librarian. For the last six years, I have been employed as a faculty librarian. During this time, I have taken leadership roles, but I have not had the opportunity to move upward into a formal management position at the community college yet. That is because the head librarian position is a rotating assignment among all full-time college librarians. The position is equivalent to other college coordinator positions and, as of the time of writing this chapter, a position has not yet become available in the library.

They Must Believe in YOU

Supervisor, manager, head, director, dean are all titles, but they mean nothing if the people you are leading don't believe in you. The positions of leadership I have acquired have been outside of my employment. These are roles I have taken because the people involved in the organization believed in me. I always believed that it is just as hard to lead a group of volunteers as it is to lead a group of employees. If you are a supervisor or are in a position of authority in a business or, in this case, an educational institution, employees know you have some sort of power. A supervisor can discipline, correct, or even fire their employees. A person in a volunteer leadership position can't do much of that, so when people elect you to be their leader, the only firing that is going to take place is if the people fire the person they elected.

How do you get people to believe in you? First, you must believe in yourself. Out of all the librarians in the country, Latin@s make up 3 percent, blacks make up 4.5 percent, Native Americans make up 1.4 percent, and Asians or Pacific Islanders make up 2.7 percent.[11] There are few minorities in the library profession, so believing in and reassuring yourself is one of those stepping stones we must take to reach leadership positions. Robin Sherma stated that to be a great leader, one must first be a great person.[12] Leaders have to find their inner strength and believe in themselves. They have to believe in what they are doing and what they want to accomplish. Nobody wants to hire a person who is always doubting themselves. Therefore, self-confidence is just as important as believing in others. The concept about believing in yourself is already built in inside many of us and was taught to us by our parents. As a Latina, my mother drilled in me and my two siblings that there was nothing that we could not accomplish.

Everything and anything is possible as long as you put your mind, soul, and sweat into it. People will also believe in you if you are honest and have a track record of fairness. Don't try to deceive others by lying about who you are and what you can accomplish. Reassure others about your ideas, and always ask for input on the things you are trying to accomplish.

Next, become part of the team and allow people to get to know you. Organizations flourish when management involves the employees and allows them to be part of the decision-making process.[13] Remember that trust between employers and employees builds better working relations.[14] People like to see action, so when you work your way up in an organization or department, people will see how you go about getting things done. If you wish to seek higher positions, you are always being watched. What you do today will affect how your boss and future subordinates think about you tomorrow, so make sure you are always using good judgment on the decisions you make. Coworkers will believe in you if you are confident. Individuals also like team players, so become involved and join in. As I mentioned before, the team player concept is very important in the work environment. Daniel Goleman explained that in the mid-1980s, 75 percent of job knowledge was stored in people's minds, and that number declined to around 20 percent because of the progression of information.[15] Therefore, people in the workplace have come to rely on each other, hence helping to continue the success of the team model. Also, remember to be honest with yourself and, most important, be honest with others. Leaders will not get far by deceiving themselves, let alone others.

MENTORING

There are many definitions for the term *mentoring*. To me, mentoring is the process of learning and taking advice from someone else. Mentors are the individuals who will provide guidance and support in order for you to develop skills to become successful. They are the ones who tell you about the dos and don'ts in the workplace, organization, or institution. I believe good mentors are able to provide their mentees with examples of strong leadership skills. In an academic library, a mentor can be a head librarian, a dean, an experienced librarian, or a senior faculty member. Upon entering your first professional position, the first thing you want to do is choose multiple mentors. Notice that I say multiple mentors and not a mentor.

The idea of choosing more than one mentor is nothing new; in the mid-1980s, this concept became very popular.[16] Management began to shift away from the idea of a top-down management style to a more independent view where responsibilities were shifted to both the boss and the subordinate.[17] Places of business began to establish mentoring programs and assign multiple mentors to workers.

A mentor can also be someone you know and admire. There is nothing wrong with having a friend or colleague as your mentor. Many times these individuals have already jumped through the hoops you are preparing to hurdle yourself. The idea of having two or three mentors allows you to learn and grab ideas from each one of them and apply those concepts to real work situations. One must keep in mind that not all mentors will be in management positions. In an academic library setting, one mentor can be a more experienced librarian, while another can be head of reference or an administrator. Also, don't be reluctant to choose a mentor if one is not assigned to you. Some academic libraries will follow an informal mentoring practice. This type of system is something that the institution might practice without a formal policy or guidelines.[18] So if your establishment does not assign you a mentor, ask several people to guide you. If a mentor is assigned to you, don't be afraid to ask another person to be an informal mentor.

Once the relationship has been established, make sure you like your mentor! I find many people talking negatively about their mentors and asking others for advice. The outcome of a negative mentor-mentee relationship could be disastrous. When a mentor-mentee relationship goes sour, a mentee's leadership growth can be underdeveloped, their self-esteem can also be affected, and even health problems can arise, like stress.[19] If you don't agree with your mentor and are having difficulty getting along with them, change mentors. But make sure that both you and the mentor have a plan in place to terminate the mentoring agreement before the start of the relationship.[20] The process of matching a mentee and mentor is crucial for the relationship to be successful. So seeking someone whom you know you can get along with is very important. Look for a person who may have the same personality characteristics as you do. Remember that a mentor should be the person you go to for problems, dilemmas, guidance, questions, or challenges. If your academic library has a formal mentoring program, make sure it too has a mentor-mentee termination clause in place. The mentoring process is designed to assist the mentee, so if you are not getting something positive from this relationship, it is time to divorce and remarry into another. Don't feel bad about changing mentors; remember that your concern should be yourself. You will not do anybody any good if you are not learning, and believe me, it will take pressure off your mentor as well. Research suggests that a negative relationship between the mentor and mentee could impact the careers of both involved with the relationship.[21] Imagine a negative mentor-mentee relationship where the mentee is asked to rate and provide feedback about their mentor. The mentee can use such information against the mentor and create a hostile environment; or vice versa, the mentor could be asked to rate their mentee. Either way can cause negative consequences, so it is in everybody's interest to have a positive mentor-mentee relationship.

GET INVOLVED AND BECOME A LEGEND

As a professional librarian, one thing I learned was to be involved within the profession. Don't be just another statistic to the library occupation; get involved and join professional organizations. However, just joining is not enough; make sure to take on responsibilities and hold important positions within the association. Start as a volunteer and move your way up the ladder. Run for important positions after you have established yourself within the organization. The American Library Association (ALA) is an excellent group that caters to all librarians, and within ALA exist numerous divisions that are great for new and tenured professionals. The Association of College and Research Libraries (ACRL) and Library Leadership and Management Association (LLAMA) are two great associations that will benefit academic librarians. ACRL is recognized as the largest division within ALA and has over 12,000 participants. According to the ACRL website, the organization is "dedicated to enhancing the ability of academic library and information professionals to serve the information needs of the higher education community and to improve learning, teaching, and research."[22] LLAMA is dedicated to helping librarians become leaders and seek management positions. LLAMA states that it "equips library professionals with tools for building vibrant and successful careers in library services."[23] These two associations are great places to start your professional development in management positions.

There are also several professional organizations for minority academic librarians. The following associations are affiliated with ALA: American Indian Library Association (AILA), Asian Pacific American Librarians Association (APALA), Black Caucus of the American Library Association (BCALA), Chinese American Librarians Association (CALA), and the National Association to Promote Library and Information Services to Latinos and the Spanish Speaking (REFORMA). There are many benefits in joining organizations of this magnitude. Ethnic, culturally driven organizations not only provide a sense of camaraderie, but also instill a passion to excel and make a difference. I am a member of REFORMA. This organization traces its roots back to 1971, when founder, Dr. Arnulfo Trejo (along with others) began to see the injustice many Spanish-speaking library users faced while visiting libraries. REFORMA began on that notion and was built on the belief that change had to come from within the profession.[24] REFORMA has a rich history of activism and perseverance. The organization is dedicated to improving the services librarians offer to the Spanish-speaking community. Executive members, chapter presidents, committee chairs, and members in general work hard to ensure that the mission and principles of REFORMA are being met. This is what I call leaders because these are the individuals who take time out of their busy lives in hopes of making a difference. Members of REFORMA join because they want to be a part of something that is good and that is making a difference in people's lives. Just this past year, REFORMA members from across the country came together and raised money to purchase children's books and deliver them to the migrant children from South America who were caught entering the United States illegally. REFORMA members did this because they cared and because it is the organization's passion that all children, regardless of their legal status, have the chance to open a book and learn. People working hard for the good of others are true leaders. The library profession is not a "work hard get rich" profession. Librarians, especially the ones in REFORMA, are educators, visionaries, and service-oriented individuals. Surrounding yourself with leaders from across the country instills a sense of camaraderie, and you realize that you are not alone in your thinking—that somewhere out there, there are like-minded people who strive to make a difference, like you.

Baseball manager Tommy Lasorda once said, "There are three kinds of people in this world: people who make it happen, people who watch what happens, and people who wonder what happened."[25] To be a leader, get involved, know what happens, and make things happen differently if you don't like what is happening. Organizations like REFORMA, AILA, APALA, CALA, and BCALA will inspire a passion in you to lead within your profession and bring much-needed change in a field that still lacks minorities. Remember to get involved with ALA, ACRL, and LLAMA. Also consider joining an ethnic-related association. These organizations are great places to start and continue your career toward a leadership position. Start at the bottom and work your way up to the top. Don't be just another member of the organization; get involved and contribute your experiences and expertise and, most important, remember to take on leadership roles. Everybody has something to share, but for it to become a story, you have to tell it, and if it's good enough, then it will eventually become a legend.

YOU DON'T NEED A TITLE TO BE A LEADER

A colleague of mine once told me that leadership needs no title. How right she was, because leadership can come in many forms. Kalin described this notion this way: "Some of the most respected librarians are those who hold neither administrative nor supervisory positions; they are simply colleagues whose voice matters and, accordingly, exert special influence on the organization."[26] I hold no official leadership title in my current role as an academic librarian. Nevertheless, that has not stopped me from taking leadership roles in order to move goals and objectives forward. The idea of leading when you are not bestowed a crown or a formal title at work should never hold you back. The best leaders are those that do not need a title to move ideas, people, or causes forward. People like Martin Luther King Jr., Susan B. Anthony, and Cesar Chavez were never given a title and a formal paycheck to lead. Instead, they searched within themselves and found the courage to fight for what was right. They were "titleless" leaders. People like them are never interested in titles; they are more interested in accomplishing goals, setting examples, and making noise. Nan Russell described the four cornerstones in her book *The Titleless Leader: How to Get Things Done When You're Not in Charge*: self-alignment, possibility seeds, soul courage, and a winning philosophy.[27] I have found some of these four traits very useful as I try to accomplish things without having a formal title. I have also used some of these theories in my volunteer work as president of the El Paso Area REFORMA Chapter and as vice president of the Texas Association of Chicanos in Higher Education (TACHE) El Paso Chapter. For example, I am a big believer in the winning philosophy cornerstone. No matter how bad things get, I always try to stay positive and keep the "we are winners" attitude alive within the organization.

People seek leaders based not on their title, but on integrity. They want someone they can count on, be inspired by, and who will deliver a positive outcome.[28] Leaders without titles also plant seeds because they believe in a group approach.[29] They see things that you might have overlooked about yourself, and most important titleless leaders believe in you.[30] Some supervisors or managers are quick to give instructions and do not allow their staff to make decisions on their own. Allowing staff to take initiative and make decisions will boost their confidence. Trusting your employees and allowing them to be a part of the team benefits the department, the supervisor, and the employee. Charles E. Watson said that management should include their subordinates as part of the team and end the *"us versus them"* attitude.[31]

Another suggestion is to always keep an eye on the "bigger picture" of things. Looking at the big picture and always thinking ahead allows you to bring the best out of people. A good leader, with or without a title, does this by identifying people's strengths and using those attributes to get things done. As a supervisor, I was good at identifying the strengths of my team members and using their talents to get things done. At the same time, my subordinates felt that their talents and expertise in certain areas were appreciated. When people recognize your talents and ask you to accomplish a task or put together a project, you feel good and go the extra mile in your work. My employees felt appreciated when they were operating a social network page, putting up a library display, or heading a small event for students. People like to be challenged and show others that they know how to get things done.

Another cornerstone described in Russell's book is soul courage.[32] A leader, whether given a title or not, must possess courage. It is not easy taking charge and delegating responsibilities, but a leader without a title must seek and use their courage to fight for what they believe in. According to Russell, being against something is not as difficult as being for something.[33] As a titleless leader, you may not have the authority to implement something you believe in or think might be beneficial for the department. Therefore, you must convince the rest to go along with you, and this requires strength and thinking autonomously. Convincing the team that your way of doing something is better than what the boss has arranged is not an easy task to accomplish. But people will soon see the sincerity you have as you seek to change the norm. People appreciate someone who is honest and fights for what they believe in. Remember that the idea is not to lead by force, but to lead those that believe in you.

A winning philosophy approach is the last cornerstone described in Russell's book that I believe is also imperative to being a successful leader.[34] Russell described this cornerstone as a "group winning" idea—if the group is winning, then the notion of the winning philosophy is accomplished.[35] Remember that a titleless leader looks at the whole picture and even plans ahead. Therefore, if the group is successful, then the mission is completed. Bad managers or supervisors many times look at end results and never bother to look at how those results came about. Good leaders, with or without a title, are just as concerned with the journey as they are with the end results. Titleless leaders want to know that the team succeeded and that everybody involved with the effort is rewarded. Many times it is more important to recognize a group for their efforts than the person who led the efforts. A team that is recognized for their attributes and is fond of their team leader will quickly recognize their trailblazer. I believe it is more important to be recognized by your own team than by a boss or an individual outside your team circle. People are more likely to remember a group of people chanting your name than an individual thanking you for your efforts.

Continue being a titleless leader when given a title as library director, dean, coordinator, or manager. Remember that titles are given by your employers, but it is your subordinates that will help you actually define what that title is, based on your performance. Titles may carry authority, but they don't always carry leadership skills. Earn your title of leadership by earning the respect of your team. The four cornerstones introduced by Nan Russell are great cornerstones to begin your titleless venture as you try to move things forward. Taking on titleless positions is a great way to improve your leadership skills. And most important, remember to search for the leader within yourself. We are all leaders inside; we just have to find that courage inside of us and give ourselves the resources to lead.

MINORITY LIBRARIANS AS LEADERS

In academic libraries, minorities represent only 13.9 percent of the total number of professionals in the field.[36] In 2006, out of the forty-seven library schools in the United States, there was only one black library director or dean, one of Asian descent, and one Latin@.[37] The numbers I just presented are not encouraging, and when I entered graduate school back in 2006, I knew about these statistics. However, instead of the numbers being a deterrent, I saw them as a challenge—a challenge to change the status quo and make a difference in the profession I had chosen. Minorities use library services, and yet the people working in libraries do not reflect the community they serve. Far worse are the numbers of minorities in leadership positions because there are only a handful of them across the country.

Past research on leadership tells us very little about underrepresented minorities in these positions. Research that has been conducted on this topic is geared more towards a Caucasian male perspective.[38] There are two models of culture leadership styles that exist; the Caucasian female and the Caucasian male.[39] Therefore, minority leaders, male or female, are many times evaluated or criticized by these standards. A person's upbringing or culture is never considered, and many times, negative labels are placed on African Americans, Latin@s, and women when they reach leadership positions.[40] According to Pegues and Cunningham, minorities are expected to behave in a certain way when they are given certain head titles.[41] So when the topic of leadership is brought forward, many people look to the existing research that tells us what and how a manager or director should behave. I have to admit that I too look for the most common things when describing the characteristics of an exceptional leader: intelligence, self-confidence, and fairness. However, I never stopped to think that these traits are actually learned while you are growing up, and not all American children are raised the same way. Pegues and Cunningham described the upbringing of Anglo youngsters differently from minority children.[42] Anglo boys are taught to be leaders, tough, and demonstrate little weakness, while Anglo girls are supposed to be more passive, dependent, and supportive.[43] African American boys and girls are taught to be strong, self-confident, and self-empowering.[44] Self-empowering is taught to young African American children because of the negative stereotypes that many black people face in this country.[45] African American children are taught to believe in themselves because many times others won't. Latin@s are brought up to respect family and respect authority.[46] This upbringing has led many Latin@s to concentrate on interpersonal skills while dealing with colleagues and management in the workplace.[47] In my own observation as a Mexican American, my brothers and I were also taught about the importance of being humble. Pegues and Cunningham described Latin@ managers and workers facing problems with this concept because at home they were taught modesty values.[48] However, in the business management world we are taught that it is okay to make yourself shine.[49] Here, I would agree with this concept to a certain extent and put aside the humility, making yourself shine and bringing attention to your accomplishments and even your efforts; however, you might want to stop short of being considered arrogant.

My philosophy has always been you do the walking and let others do the talking. Instead of speaking about yourself and the degrees you hold, talk about the goals you want to accomplish. Let people know about the exciting project you are working on within your library. A secret I'll share with you is to accomplish something and make sure it makes its way to the public. Ask a good friend to write something about you on a blog or newsletter. If no blog exists, start one for your library. Blogs are a great way to tell people about the accomplishments, rewards, and efforts you and your department are working on or have completed. These tactics are acceptable because you should be proud of your accomplishments. At the same time, give credit where credit is deserved. If you belong to a group that has accomplished something big, give credit to the group and make sure people know you are part of the team.

The importance of equality was another thing my parents drilled in me and my brothers. Both my parents were born in Mexico and both faced discrimination and racism when they came to the United States. During the early 1970s, my parents were once refused service in a Denny's restaurant in Phoenix, Arizona. According to my mother, who happened to be blonde with green eyes, in those days' white women were looked down upon for dating nonwhite men. Little did they know that my mom was born in Mexico; nevertheless, the refusal of service further ignited my parents to teach their children about the importance of tolerance and self-pride. Like many Latin@s we are a very proud people and have never denied our background or culture. Today, I teach the same things to my children: be proud of their heritage, their language, and the last name that they carry. Having a sense of pride about your own culture allows you to respect other cultures and ethnicities.

Different childhood lessons, along with our education and life experiences, create the kind of leaders we will be in the future. Recall your upbringing and, if possible, ask your parents or older siblings about the way you were raised. These important factors build who you are, and many times without knowing; use these influences to make decisions that will lead to leadership positions. At the same time, learn the leadership traits and models that currently exist. Yes, these practices are based on beliefs and experiences of Caucasian men, but if minorities refuse to learn what they have done and accomplished, then how can we compete? You must learn how to play the game first in order to compete in it and eventually change it. Don't be afraid to bring your ideology and philosophy into the leadership model literature. Remember, this is an area that has not been fully researched; it is up to minorities to write the next chapter of the different leadership models that exist.

So where are these minority leaders? We are here! In reference to my previous section about leaders without titles, some minority librarians are leaders but without a title. Many of us have already "infiltrated" the library profession as library clerks, professional academic librarians, professors, deans, and directors. Although we are small in numbers within the profession, I believe that minorities develop leadership traits growing up that non-minorities may never experience. People of color have to work extra hard to get ahead in life because discrimination, racism, and negative stereotypes still exist. Yet somehow African Americans, Latin@s and other ethnic groups have been able to prevail. Many of us are leaders in our families because we are the first to go to college; others are seen as leaders in their communities because they champion change. Many times minorities are put in difficult situations dealing with racism, and somehow we have learned to either cope, ignore, or fight back about it. Either way, leadership development skills are being built as we go through life experiences.

CONCLUSION

Statistics paint a picture of what society looks like, but the good thing with stats is that they can be transformed. Use your culture and upbringing as tools and resources on how to lead. Remember that the odds have been stacked up against us as minorities. Use what you have learned at home, at school, and at work to move your leadership agenda forward. Also keep in mind that it is acceptable to talk about yourself and to share the wonderful things you are doing and are planning to accomplish; just remember to be modest.

Leaders are not born; they are created. A slogan I made years ago as an undergraduate student and member of Moviemental Estudianti Chicano/a de Aztlan (MEChA) states that "We shall not search for leaders; we will create them." There is no such thing as a natural leader. Many of us romanticize the idea and believe that leaders are born, but the reality is that they are created. Leaders are actually "born" from organizations, business departments, social groups, professions, athletic teams, and even from the clique we hung out with during our youth. The process of leadership begins with mentoring—people giving you a sense of direction or advice on *how to, where,* and *why* things are done in a certain way. Believe in yourself and have confidence in yourself as you accomplish tasks. Titles are good to hold, but they mean nothing if the people you are leading do not believe in you. Mentors provide a vast amount of knowledge, such as the ins and outs of the department or the culture of the work area. Mentors are there to catch you when you fall, but most important, to help you back on your feet. Remember to be involved with professional organizations; those that rise to the top within the association are recognized. These organizations are also fun, and the people you meet and the accomplishments you do will last a lifetime. The library career itself is hungry for the next leader that will take the profession to the next level. Maybe it's you? Neither you nor I will ever know unless you become involved. You don't need a title to start showing your leadership traits. Recall the four cornerstones that Russell suggested in her book. These four cornerstones are excellent ideas to learn as you start preparing for your future management role. The statistics of minority academic library leaders are few, but don't let this prevent your quest to become a library head someday. Use what you have learned and the experiences you and your family have gone through as a tool to lead. Your upbringing and cultural values built who you are today, so appreciate them and use them to your benefit. My identity as a Latino has grounded me and motivated me to continue to work hard regardless of the title that I hold.

NOTES

1.   Pew Research Center, "Race in America: Tracking 50 Years of Demographic Trends," August 22, 2013, http://www.pewsocialtrends.org/2013/08/22/race-demographics/.

2.   "Complaint Alleges Shocking Bias at General Electric," *HR Specialist: New York Employment Law* 8, no. 2 (February 2013): 5, Business Source Complete, EBSCOhost, 92971881.

3.   Clare O'Connor, "Perfumania, Maker of Donald Trump Fragrances, Cuts Ties with Mogul," *Forbes*, July 9, 2015: 15, Business Source Complete, EBSCOhost, 108266908.

4.   Sharon Elteto, Rose M. Jackson, and Adriene Lim, "Is the Library a 'Welcoming Space'? An Urban Academic Library and Diverse Student Experiences," *portal: Libraries and the Academy* 8, no. 3 (July 2008): 325–37, doi:10.1353/pla.0.0008.

5.   C. Shawn Burke, Linda G. Pierce, and Eduardo Salas, *Understanding Adaptability* (Amsterdam: Elsevier JAI, 2006), eBook Collection, 166850.

6.   Laurence Shatkin, *200 Best Jobs for Introverts* (Indianapolis, IN: JIST Publishing, 2008), 13.

7.   Sondra Thiederman, "Distorted Vision: Knowing Your Own Culture in Order to Know Others" (reprinted with permission), Diversity News, Human Resource Professionals of Minnesota, 2014, http://www.hrpmn.org/?66.

8.   Adrian Schoo, "Leaders and Their Teams: Learning to Improve Performance with Emotional Intelligence and Using Choice Theory," *International Journal of Reality Therapy* 27, no. 2 (Spring 2008): 40, Psychology and Behavioral Sciences Collection, EBSCOhost, 31818868.

9.   Ibid., 40.

10. Charles E. Watson, *How Honesty Pays* (Westport, CT: Praeger, 2005).

11. Mark Winston, "Managing Diversity," *Library Leadership and Management* 24, no. 3 (June 2010): 62, Library & Information Source, EBSCOhost, 51487362.

12. Robin Sharma, *The Leader Who Had No Title* (New York: Free Press, 2010), 161.

13. Watson, *How Honesty Pays*, 146.

14. Ibid.

15. Daniel Goleman, *Working with Emotional Intelligence* (New York: Bantam Books, 1998), 203.

16. Ann Manning Fiegen, "Mentoring and Academic Librarians: Personally Designed for Results," *College and Undergraduate Libraries* 9, no. 1 (June 2002): 23–32, doi:10.1300/J106v09n01_03.

17. Ibid., 25.

18. Marni R. Harrington, and Elizabeth Marshall, "Analyses of Mentoring Expectations, Activities, and Support in Canadian Academic Libraries," *College and Research Libraries* 75, no. 6 (November 2014): 763–90. doi:10.5860/crl.75.6.763.

19. Deborah Hicks, "The Practice of Mentoring: Reflecting on the Critical Aspects for Leadership Development," *Australian Library Journal* 60, no. 1 (February 2011): 66–74, Library & Information Science Source, EBSCOhost, 67021095.

20. Ibid., 73.
21. Ibid., 68.
22. American Library Association, "Association of College and Research Libraries," dynamically generated page, accessed January 29, 2015, http://www.ala.org/acrl/index.php.
23. American Library Association, "About LLAMA," accessed February 3, 2015, http://www.ala.org/llama/about.
24. Salvador Güereña and Edward Erazo, "Latinos and Librarianship," *Library Trends* 49, no. 1 (Summer 2000): 138–81. Academic Search Complete, EBSCOhost, 3792444.
25. Tommy Lasorda, "Tommy Lasorda Quotes," BrainyQuote.com, accessed March 8, 2015, http://www.brainyquote.com/quotes/quotes/t/tommylasor610901.html.
26. Sally W. Kalin, "Reframing Leadership: The ACRL/Harvard Leadership Institute for Academic Librarians," *Journal of Business and Finance Librarianship* 13, no. 3 (March 2008): 262 doi:10.1080/08963560802183047.
27. Nan S. Russell, *The Titleless Leader* (Pompton Plains, NJ: Career Press, 2012).
28. Ibid., 123.
29. Ibid., 124.
30. Ibid.
31. Watson, *How Honesty Pays*, 146.
32. Russell, *Titleless Leader*, 126.
33. Ibid., 127.
34. Ibid., 128.
35. Ibid.
36. American Library Association, "Diversity Counts 2009–2010 Update," September 18, 2012, http://www.ala.org/offices/diversity/diversitycounts/2009–2010update.
37. Robin Sharma, "Diversity and Equality in Library and Information Science (LIS) Recruitment, Education, and Readiness," *Library Times International: World News Digest of Library and Information Science* 22, no. 4 (April 2006): 29–30, Library & Information Science Source, EBSCOhost, 20753294.
38. Demarcus A. Pegues and Christopher J. L. Cunningham, "Diversity in Leadership: Where's the Love for Racioethnic Minorities?" *Business Journal of Hispanic Research* 4, no. 1 (2010), Business Source Complete, EBSCOhost, 50375695.
39. Ibid., 14.
40. Ibid.
41. Ibid., 13.
42. Ibid., 14.
43. Ibid., 14–15.
44. Ibid., 15.
45. Ibid.
46. Ibid.
47. Ibid.

48. Ibid.
49. Ibid.

Bibliography

American Library Association. "About LLAMA." Accessed February 3, 2015. http://www.ala.org/llama/about.

———. "Association of College and Research Libraries." Dynamically generated page, accessed January 29, 2015. http://www.ala.org/acrl/index.php.

———. "Diversity Counts 2009–2010 Update." September 18, 2012. http://www.ala.org/offices/diversity/diversitycounts/2009–2010update.

Burke, C. Shawn, Linda G. Pierce, and Eduardo Salas. *Understanding Adaptability: A Prerequisite for Effective Performance within Complex Environments.* Amsterdam: Elsevier JAI, 2006. eBook Collection,166850. EBSCOhost.

"Complaint Alleges Shocking Bias at General Electric." *HR Specialist: New York Employment Law* 8, no. 2 (February 2013): 5. Business Source Complete, EBSCOhost, 92971881.

Elteto, Sharon, Rose M. Jackson, and Adriene Lim. "Is the Library a 'Welcoming Space'? An Urban Academic Library and Diverse Student Experiences." *portal: Libraries and the Academy* 8, no. 3 (July 2008): 325–37. doi:10.1353/pla.0.0008.

Fiegen, Ann Manning. "Mentoring and Academic Librarians: Personally Designed for Results." *College and Undergraduate Libraries* 9, no. 1 (June 2002): 23–32. doi:10.1300/J106v09n01_03.

Goleman, Daniel. *Working with Emotional Intelligence.* New York: Bantam Books, 1998.

Güereña, Salvador, and Edward Erazo. "Latinos and Librarianship." *Library Trends* 49, no. 1 (Summer 2000): 138–81. Academic Search Complete, EBSCOhost, 3792444.

Harrington, Marni R., and Elizabeth Marshall. "Analyses of Mentoring Expectations, Activities, and Support in Canadian Academic Libraries." *College and Research Libraries* 75, no. 6 (November 2014): 763–90. doi:10.5860/crl.75.6.763.

Hicks, Deborah. "The Practice of Mentoring: Reflecting on the Critical Aspects for Leadership Development." *Australian Library Journal* 60, no. 1 (February 2011): 66–74. Library & Information Science Source, EBSCOhost, 67021095.

Kalin, Sally W. "Reframing Leadership: The ACRL/Harvard Leadership Institute for Academic Librarians." *Journal of Business and Finance Librarianship* 13, no. 3 (March 2008): 261–70. doi:10.1080/08963560802183047.

Lasorda, Tommy. "Tommy Lasorda Quotes." BrainyQuote.com. Accessed March 8, 2015. http://www.brainyquote.com/quotes/quotes/t/tommylasor610901.html.

O'Connor, Clare. "Perfumania, Maker of Donald Trump Fragrances, Cuts Ties with Mogul." *Forbes,* July 9, 2015: 15. Business Source Complete, EBSCOhost, 108266908.

Pegues, Demarcus A., and Christopher J. L. Cunningham. "Diversity in Leadership: Where's the Love for Racioethnic Minorities?" *Business Journal of Hispanic Research* 4, no. 1 (2010). Business Source Complete, EBSCOhost, 50375695.

Pew Research Center. "Race in America: Tracking 50 Years of Demographic Trends." August 22, 2013. http://www.pewsocialtrends.org/2013/08/22/race-demographics/.

Russell, Nan S. *The Titleless Leader: How to Get Things Done When You're Not in Charge.* Pompton Plains, NJ: Career Press, 2012.

Schoo, Adrian. "Leaders and Their Teams: Learning to Improve Performance with Emotional Intelligence and Using Choice Theory." *International Journal of Reality Therapy* 27, no. 2 (Spring 2008): 40–45. Psychology and Behavioral Sciences Collection, EBSCOhost, 31818868.

Sharma, Robin. "Diversity and Equality in Library and Information Science (LIS) Recruitment, Education, and Readiness." *Library Times International: World News Digest of Library and Information Science* 22, no. 4 (April 2006): 29–30. Library & Information Science Source, EBSCOhost, 20753294.

———. *The Leader Who Had No Title: A Modern Fable on Real Success in Business and in Life.* New York: Free Press, 2010.

Shatkin, Laurence. *200 Best Jobs for Introverts.* Indianapolis, IN: JIST Publishing, 2008.

Thiederman, Sondra. "Distorted Vision: Knowing Your Own Culture in Order to Know Others." Reprinted with permission. Diversity News, Human Resource Professionals of Minnesota. 2014. http://www.hrpmn.org/?66.

Watson, Charles E. *How Honesty Pays: Restoring Integrity to the Workplace.* Westport, CT: Praeger, 2005.

Winston, Mark "Managing Diversity." *Library Leadership and Management* 24, no. 3 (June 2010): 58–63. Library & Information Source, EBSCOhost, 51487362.

Chapter 3

LEADERSHIP BEGINS WITH YOU

Shannon D. Jones

MY LOVE OF libraries and learning was nurtured by my grandmother, who was born on a farm and had a seventh-grade education. My grandmother was born in 1913 during a period when African Americans were not allowed to pursue an education and their career options were limited. As a result, she had an insatiable desire to see all of her grandchildren get an education and do well in life. For her, the key to success was to harness those things that were rightfully yours regardless of your socioeconomic status. No one could take away your ability to pursue an education, a love for reading, or the right to use a library. My grandmother bought me my first book and instilled in me a love of reading. She encouraged me to not take people at face value. As she used to say, "You are smart enough to look for your own answers and make your decisions based on what you have learned." During her formidable years, my grandmother was told that the best way to keep information from someone, in her case from a black person, was to put it in a book. I have held those words close to my heart since I was a child. In fact, those words first inspired me to pursue a career as a librarian.

My mother also influenced my decision to become a librarian. She instilled in me the importance of not comparing myself to others. In her words, "You are not them. You are YOU!" She taught me to have an un-wavering confidence in my ability to do anything that I wanted to do and to pursue my goals relentlessly regardless of what other people thought or said. One of the many invaluable life lessons she stressed to me was that I had to live with the consequences of the decisions I made. She instilled in me the importance of seeking advice as necessary, but I should make decisions for myself, especially about those things that would have long-lasting implications.

Both of these beautiful women left traditions and legacies that I carry with me always. I've incorporated everything that I learned from my mother and grandmother into my own identity as a woman, a librarian, and a leader. From this context, I offer what I consider to be best practices for bringing out the leader in you and being the best librarian possible.

I pursued librarianship with the overarching goal of becoming the best librarian I could be. In my mind, the fact that I am African American should not make a difference in whether I'm successful or not, though it might make my journey to becoming the best a little harder. Indeed, the occasional struggle or setback, once overcome, has made me a better person and librarian. As a first-generation college student, I entered the profession understanding that being mediocre was not an option. I knew that I needed a plan, the wherewithal to execute that plan, and the confidence to walk in my success. I also understood that on my journey, I would meet people who could help me along the way, and I had to be smart enough to recognize and accept help. Knowing that I am now in the position to offer help to others, I offer the following strategies for developing a career in librarianship and negotiating the world of leadership.

DEFINE AND PURSUE A LEADERSHIP VISION

As you begin to think about becoming a leader in our profession, you should consider several things: Leadership begins with you. In fact, all leadership begins with self-leadership. In Peter Drucker's article "Managing Oneself," he stated that you cannot begin to lead other people if you are not leading yourself effectively.[1] Essentially you have to decide what type of leader you want to be. The best way to do this is by defining and pursuing a leadership vision for yourself. As with any goal, you must conceive the vision before you can achieve the vision. Take time to reflect on your personal leadership vision by asking the following questions: What do you want to achieve in your career? Where do you want to be in five to ten years? What are you willing to sacrifice to reach your goals? What values are central to you and to who you are? These questions will help you do several things: (1) define your vision, (2) develop the vision, (3) defend and communicate the vision, and (4) demonstrate the vision.

Lee and King also suggested that you should develop a personal and a leadership vision. The personal vision should do three things: incorporate your dreams and passions, be authentic and true to your realities, and evolve continually.[2] They also noted, "Your leadership vision needs to be grounded in your personal vision. Your personal vision serves your leadership vision in a very important way: it lets you know what leadership roles to accept or decline, seek or avoid."[3] To help you clarify your personal vision, Lee and King suggested that you "look at yourself in one or more of the following ways: tell your own story, reflect on your daydreams, look for patterns in events, behaviors, focus, and energy, take lessons from role models, assess how you feel about power, assess your responses to conflict, note your creative environment, and follow your intuition."[4]

Once you establish your leadership vision, you must then set realistic priorities to help you move strategically toward your vision. Seek out those people and programs that may help you along the way. As you develop your vision, you should also read the library literature, as well as that of other disciplines, such as business and education. What skills and attributes does library literature suggest are core competencies for library leaders? You will find that you may already have some of the required skills.

CREATE YOUR OWN CAREER ROAD MAP

One of the lessons that I learned in grade school is that proper planning prevents poor preparation. In a nutshell, being successful in this profession requires that you be intentional and willing to invest in your own development. Your willingness to invest the time, energy, and attention in crafting a successful career in librarianship depends on you. You have to take ownership of your own development.

Year after year, libraries and other organizations develop strategic plans to serve as a road map for where they are going in the future. These plans set goals and identify specific actions to achieve those goals. As librarians, we should undergo the same process for developing our careers; we should each have a personal strategic plan for our careers. Achieving excellence and being the best at anything takes planning, preparation, and persistence. We must be intentional and willing to invest in our own development. My success as a librarian did not happen overnight; it is the result of having a laser-focused plan, well-thought-out decisions and follow-through. Every development opportunity I've completed, advanced degree I've earned, leadership institute or program I've attended, coupled with the practical experience that I've gained has been strategically selected to advance me toward my goals.

One strategy that works for me is to identify long- and short-term goals for myself. I tend to plan my life out in three-year intervals. Career planning or development is similar to website development. One of the things that we often hear about websites is that they are works in progress, always under construction. I like to apply this analogy to career development. You are a work in progress and, as such, you should always be thinking of ways to improve your skill set, enhance your marketability, and improve your brand. The best way that I've found to do this is to develop a strategic plan for your career. It will serve as your plan of action for achieving your professional goals.

One of the first questions often asked in strategic planning meetings is, "What's our brand?" A librarian, then, might ask herself the same question: What is my skill set? How am I unique? How might those skills and talents drive the direction of my career? Once you answer these questions, you can identify your long- and short-term goals. This strategy of setting long- and short-term goals has been key to my success.

A key question to ask as you begin to plan your career goals is what it is you need to achieve your long-term goals. As Revelle noted, "If you have a long-term career goal, you must prepare yourself to reach that goal through a combination of education, experience and networking."[5] For example, when I decided that my long-term goal was to become a library director, I set a series of short-term goals that would move me toward that larger goal. First, I began to study librarians who held directorships at that time. I reviewed their credentials, explored professional development opportunities, observed my library directors at work, and got to know several directors. These steps helped me better understand the types of goals I needed to set. I also did a Strengths, Weaknesses, Opportunities, and Threats (SWOT) Analysis to identify my strengths and weaknesses. According to Hansen and Hansen, a SWOT analysis focuses on the "internal and external environments, examining strengths and weaknesses in the internal environment and opportunities and threats in the external environment."[6] They suggested that you "examine your current situation by asking the following: What are your strengths and weaknesses? How can you capitalize on your strengths and overcome your weaknesses? What are the external opportunities and threats in your chosen career field?"[7] By identifying these characteristics, I was able to better understand not only who I was but how I could predict the barriers I would face and develop strategies to overcome them.

In the previous paragraph, I encouraged you to set long-term goals for your career. Setting short-term goals is equally important. For example, once I achieved my goal of becoming a library director, I set several short-term goals that I believed would help me to be successful during my first year. Examples of short-term goals I set for myself include shadowing three directors in my first year, identifying and completing a leadership development opportunity for new leaders or library directors, attending a fund-raising conference, and exercising three times a week. Setting short-term goals will allow you to reach small, impactful milestones as you work toward your long-term goals. More importantly, reaching milestones builds confidence.

In 2005, I had the opportunity to participate in the Minnesota Institute for Early Career Librarians from Traditionally Underrepresented Groups. One of our assigned readings was Peter Drucker's article "Managing Oneself." In the article, Drucker stated, "We must each be our own chief executive officer. He says "it's up to you to carve out your place in the work world and know when to change course."[8] The key takeaway from this article is, "All leadership begins with self-leadership."[9] You cannot begin to lead others if you have not mastered the art of leading yourself. The idea of carving out my own future resonated with me and has stuck with me ever since.

GET A MENTOR

At the 2015 Midwinter Meeting of the American Library Association, I had the opportunity to have an informal conversation with the university librarian from one of my previous libraries. As we rode the shuttle to the convention center, I thanked him for helping to nurture and advance my career over the previous ten years. I also shared with him how much I appreciated the opportunity to observe and learn from him. I realized that much of the knowledge and many of the skills I use in my current position I learned from watching him lead our library system. For me, he was an unacknowledged role model. I characterize this librarian as an "unacknowledged" role model because, until that conversation at Midwinter, I had never expressed to him my appreciation for him being an excellent leader. I appreciated his business acumen, his professionalism, and his overall approach to leadership. I have many mentors, and they are all impactful in my development in some way. I encourage you to look around the profession. There are numerous leaders in librarianship. Before seeking out a mentor, set clear goals of what you would like to get out of the relationship. You want to be mentored by someone who will give you honest, authentic feedback about ideas and strategies.

As you progress in your career, you will find that you have different mentors for different purposes. In addition, depending on the nature of the goal that you set with your mentor, your interaction with that person may be long- or short-term. Some mentoring relationships naturally happen over time, while others are part of formal leadership programs. While there are benefits to formal mentoring, the literature suggests that "informal mentoring provides opportunities for a personalized approach, yet maintains enough flexibility to prevent participants from viewing the process as rigid or stagnant."[10] I have found this to be true in my own mentoring relationships.

Additional benefits of having a mentor include "receiving both help and direction from the mentor in a collaborative manner."[11] For example, as a new librarian, I had a seasoned librarian take me under her wing, helping me navigate the complex university landscape and learn the ropes. This was extremely important for me as a new librarian and as a minority. Essentially, she assisted me with swimming rather than watching me sink. As a minority librarian, I always have a subconscious feeling that all eyes are on me, especially in situations where I am the sole minority in a leadership role. In fact, it is not uncommon to feel as if you have to be smarter and work harder than everyone in the room to be taken seriously and to prove that you have what it takes to do the job effectively. It is especially important that minority librarians seek out mentors. Research indicates "that librarians of color often feel isolated, intimidated, and alienated due to joining a predominantly white profession where others may be older and have more job-related experience."[12] Ross suggested that the benefits of mentoring minorities include "instilling confidence and providing minorities with a set of skills with which they can compete in a high-pressure workplace. These skills might include publication and presentation advice or more practical skills that allow minority librarians a better understanding of the politics and environment of an academic organization."[13] Overall, mentoring is important for your professional development. As you benefit from your mentor's guidance, you are also preparing to become a mentor to those who will need your guidance in the future.

PRACTICE SELF-REFLECTION

A key concept that I learned and practiced while working on my master's in education was the importance of self-reflection as a learning process. The impact of reflection during my graduate studies was so influential that I continue to use it as a key aspect of my professional practice. Self-reflection has ultimately made me a stronger leader. As a leader, I have learned to be both thoughtful and intentional about the decisions I make and the projects that I take on. Murdoch-Eaton and Sandars wrote that "reflection is an essential aspect of all of our lives. We have an experience, we think about why we reacted in a certain way and we then consider whether we need to take action and alter our response to similar experiences in the future."[14] I have found this advice to be true.

For example, as a manager it is my goal to make well-thought-out decisions with the library's best interest in mind. Sometimes I get this right, but then there are those times when the unexpected happens and no matter what I have done the outcome could not have been improved. At these times, reflection is the most important. Each and every time I make a decision that does not yield the desired outcome, I retreat to my quiet place and ask myself the following questions: (1) What could I have done differently to change the outcome? (2) If given an opportunity for a do-over, would I actually do something different? (3) What are my lessons learned? and (4) Did the world end? If the world didn't end as a result of my decision, I normally take my lessons learned and move on. I have found this process to be particularly helpful when having difficult conversations. Roberts and Westville noted that "one cannot possibly study ahead of time how to handle every situation that may present itself, but one can develop a process of learning from experience that ensures progressive competency development over time."[15] While there are many benefits to self-reflection, the major benefit acknowledged by Murdoch-Eaton and Sandars is that reflection is "a deliberate process of thinking about a typical complex experience after the event [that] has the potential to improve intuitive professional decision making."[16]

As Plack and colleagues noted, "Reflection, as a method of learning from experience, has been widely accepted in various domains of professional education."[17] I believe this is true of librarianship as well, so I encourage you to make self-reflection a part of your professional practice. You might use several strategies to incorporate reflection into your professional practice. For example, you may find it helpful to write your thoughts in a journal or engage in dialogue with a trusted colleague, mentor, or friend. I tend to use a combination of the two, as both have their benefits. Sharing your reflection via dialogue will allow you to "hear an alternate perspective, challenge you to think critically, and to develop collaborative reflective skills necessary for participation in learning organizations".[18] Alternatively, writing your reflections in a journal will allow you to review your reflection at a later date to see how your thoughts and behaviors have evolved over time.

BE AN AGENT OF CHANGE

One of my favorite quotes from Mahatma Gandhi is, "Be the change you want to see in the world." Gandhi knew that a change agent must model the behavior that she wants to see from those impacted by the change. By modeling inspirational behavior, the change agent gains influence because people respect a leader who does more than give lip service to a given change.

A change agent knows that change is constant and a leader can either lead that change or be left behind. Throughout my lifetime, I've dealt with a variety of change initiatives that have impacted not only how I accomplish tasks personally and professionally, but also how I respond. From these experiences, I've learned that change is not only constant, but that it comes in many shapes and forms: change can be planned, but oftentimes it's unanticipated; people accept change at different rates; people will either embrace change or resist it at all costs; growth cannot happen without change; and not all change is bad. It has been in moments of immense and often intense change that I've found my voice, pursued a passion, fulfilled a dream, or discovered a talent.

Finally, as you deal with change in your career, I recommend having your own method for deciding when to fight or embrace a change. One thing that has kept me grounded has been Reinhold Niebuhr's "Serenity Prayer," which reads, "God grant me the serenity to accept the things I cannot change, the courage to change the things I can, and the wisdom to know the difference." I've said this prayer on countless occasions at work and at home. It helps me to focus my energies and attentions in the right direction and on the right priorities. The prayer reminds me that as a change agent, my goal is to focus my energies on impacting those things that are within my power to control. More importantly, it helps me to achieve a peaceful mind-set in the face of adversity, turmoil, chaos, and uncertainty. I encourage you to find your serenity.

Take Care of Your Mind and Body

I liken the responsibilities of being a leader to those of a caregiver. As leader you will spend a tremendous amount of time caring for the interests of the library and your staff. You can perhaps do this best by doing what the old adage says and trying to put yourself in their shoes. However, in order to be most effective at giving care, a leader must also ensure that she is getting adequate self-care. I learned the value of caring for your mind and body after my first week as a new library director. At the conclusion of my first week in my new position, I found myself mentally and physically tired, exhausted in fact. I learned immediately that to do this job effectively would require an increased level of physical and mental stamina. As I reflected on my first week, I realized that my schedule was stacked so tightly that I had meetings scheduled through my normal lunchtime hour. My advice to you is to be intentional about planning time away from work to allow yourself time to reset. For me, this meant that I needed to make sure that I allocated time to take lunch every day or to get out of the library and walk around campus. Bolman and Gallos offered five steps for being a healthy academic leader, arguing that

> healthy leaders care for self and build vitality by attending to boundaries, biology, balance, beauty, and bounce:
>
> **Boundaries**—Distinguish between their own business and the baggage and work of others, **Biology**—Remaining vigilant to boundary management takes concentration and stamina that are strengthened by conscious attention to self-care and good health; **Balance**—retaining one's equilibrium and perspective in the face of challenge or frustration; **Beauty**—Identify activities and events that feed the soul, and **Bounce**—the ability to adapt and strengthen in the face of challenge, trauma, or stress.[19]

Successful leadership should not come at the expense of your physical or mental health. You will not be able to lead people toward your vision if you are not able to physically or mentally withstand the pressures of your leadership role. Do what you can to take care of yourself. I have found that the fastest road to burnout is to neglect your own well-being.

CONCLUSION

Being successful as a library leader requires that you take intentional steps towards achieving your leadership goals. In this chapter, I offered several strategies that have worked for me, including encouraging you to define and pursue a leadership vision; creating a road map to chart your leadership path; getting a mentor whom you can consult for advice; practicing self-reflection so that you learn from your experiences, good or bad; being a change agent; and taking care of your mind and body so that you don't lose yourself in the work. These strategies have helped me build a foundation for greatness. I hope you will use these same strategies to propel you forward in your leadership endeavors.

Notes

1. Peter Drucker, "Managing Oneself," *Harvard Business Review* 83, no. 1 (2005): 100–9.
2. Robert J. Lee and Sara N. King, *Discovering the Leader in You* (San Francisco: Jossey-Bass, 2001).
3. Ibid., 34. Center for Academic Excellence and The Writing Center.
4. Ibid., 37.
5. Jack B. Revelle, "Call a SPADE a SPADE," *Quality Progress* 44, no. 3 (2011): 54.
6. Randall S. Hansen and Katharine Hansen, "Using a SWOT Analysis in Your Career Planning," *Quintessential Careers QuintZine* 1, no. 16 (October 9, 2000), https://www.livecareer.com/quintessential/swot-analysis.
7. Ibid.
8. Drucker, "Managing Oneself," 1.
9. Ibid. 1.
10. Kevin M. Ross, "Purposeful Mentoring in Academic Libraries," *Journal of Library Administration* 53, no. 7–8 (2013): 416.
11. Ibid., 417.
12. Ibid., 418.
13. Ibid., 418.
14. Deborah Murdoch-Eaton and John Sandars, "Reflection: Moving from a Mandatory Ritual to Meaningful Professional Development," *Archives of Disease in Childhood* 99, no. 3 (2014): 279.
15. Cynthia Roberts and I. N. Westville, "Developing Future Leaders: The Role of Reflection in the Classroom," *Journal of Leadership Education* 7, no. 1 (2008):117.
16. Murdoch-Eaton and Sandars, "Reflection," 279.
17. Margaret M. Plack, Maryanne Driscoll, Sylvene Blissett, Raymond McKenna, and Thomas P. Plack, "A Method for Assessing Reflective Journal Writing," *Journal of Allied Health* 34, no. 4 (2005): 199.
18. Roberts and Westville, "Developing Future Leaders," 121.
19. Lee G. Bolman and Joan V. Gallos, *Reframing Academic Leadership* (Hoboken, NJ: John Wiley and Sons, 2010), 191–197.

Bibliography

Bolman, Lee G., and Joan V. Gallos. *Reframing Academic Leadership.* Hoboken, NJ: John Wiley and Sons, 2010.

Drucker, Peter F. "Managing Oneself." *Harvard Business Review* 83, no. 1 (2005): 1–12.

Hansen, Randall S., and Katharine Hansen. "Using a SWOT Analysis in Your Career Planning." *Quintessential Careers QuintZine* 1, no. 16 (October 9, 2000). https://www.livecareer.com/quintessential/swot-analysis.

Lee, Robert J., and Sara N. King. *Discovering the Leader in You: A Guide to Realizing Your Personal Leadership Potential.* San Francisco: Jossey-Bass, 2001.

Murdoch-Eaton, Deborah, and John Sandars. "Reflection: Moving from a Mandatory Ritual to Meaningful Professional Development." *Archives of Disease in Childhood* 99, no. 3 (2014): 279–83.

Plack, Margaret M., Maryanne Driscoll, Sylvene Blissett, Raymond McKenna, and Thomas P. Plack. "A Method for Assessing Reflective Journal Writing." *Journal of Allied Health* 34, no. 4 (2005): 199–208.

Revelle, Jack B. "Call a SPADE a SPADE." *Quality Progress* 44, no. 3 (2011): 54.

Roberts, Cynthia, and I. N. Westville. "Developing Future Leaders: The Role of Reflection in the Classroom." *Journal of Leadership Education* 7, no. 1 (2008): 116–30.

Ross, Kevin M. "Purposeful Mentoring in Academic Libraries." *Journal of Library Administration* 53, no. 7–8 (2013): 412–28.

Chapter 4

Can You Be a "Troublemaker" without "Making Trouble"?

Reflections on Self-Development, Self-Acceptance, and Unsettling the Racialized Workplace in the Most Productive Possible Way

Michelle Baildon

LIKE MANY LIBRARIANS, I "fell into" this career, but looking back, I can see all the signs—it was just meant to be. The first and clearest indication was the career interest assessment I took my freshman year that gave "librarian" as the best match (I reacted with complete bafflement). Right from my first semester, my favorite reply when anyone asked me what I liked best about my university was "The libraries." And when I was in grad school for American studies, I sent suggestions of books from my race theory class to my high school librarian—who is still a dear friend—for consideration for the school's collection. I just couldn't help myself; I'd never even heard of "collection development," but it was already a compulsion. It seems funny to me now that it took me as long as it did to get this figured out.

My self-conception as a "leader" has similarly come to me gradually over the years, and in fits and starts. I can look back and see the raw material—in need of much development and refinement—even going back to my high school days (and with much more development and refinement still to come). It took several stints as an elected officer in two professional associations, the Asian Pacific American Librarians Association (APALA) and the RUSA History Section, as well as eighteen months as a participant in the invaluable ARL Leadership Career Development Program (LCDP), for this self-conception to begin to crystallize.

Because this was a somewhat slow and indirect realization, I can't say that I developed conscious strategies during most of my career to engage my internal leadership drive. I understand now, however, that from the beginning of my career, I thought a lot about how things could be better and tried my best to influence my organization to change. Consciously or not, I made choices that sustained this impulse and that put me in contexts where I could plan, influence, coordinate, direct, and make decisions in an effort to improve things for colleagues and patrons. I'm now able to look back and articulate these choices as strategies; I hope they might help other librarians of color maintain motivation for and commitment to leadership.

FIRST, SOME CONTEXT: ASIAN AMERICANS AND LEADERSHIP

In recent years, I've been interested in research and discussion about obstacles faced by Asian Americans in the workplace, which in aggregate present a barrier to advancement that's been called the "bamboo ceiling." Asian Americans are disproportionately poorly represented in elected office, upper management of corporations, high-level administration in higher education, and as leaders of other types of organizations.[1] The disparity is particularly notable in Silicon Valley, where a 2015 study of five large technology companies found that although 27 percent of professionals employed by the companies were Asian or Asian American, they constituted less than 19 percent of managers and less than 14 percent of executives.[2] As management professor Lei Lai points out, "In both public and private sectors, Asian Americans have the lowest probability to be promoted to managerial positions among all racial minorities and have a lower ratio of managers to professionals and a lower return to education compared with Whites."[3]

This underrepresentation flies in the face of the model minority myth, which inaccurately posits Asian Americans as the ideal American success story. Asian Americans are stereotyped as a group with disproportionately high levels of educational, economic, and social attainment, all based on hard work and sound cultural values. This myth obscures the tremendous variety of histories and experiences within the category of "Asian American" and minimizes the systemic racism faced by Asian Americans and by all people of color in the United States. The underlying assumption is that if Asian Americans can make it, why not other people of color? It's a rhetorical tool used to deny the existence of racism as a structural barrier in the United States, as well as a means to create division between Asian Americans and other people of color. And this myth lives on despite the fact that, in many ways, Asian Americans are *not* actually making it.

Social scientists as well as human resources and industry consultants have offered a variety of explanations for this workplace leadership disparity. Psychologists focus on interpersonal dynamics of individuals at work, looking for differences between perceptions of Asian Americans and Caucasians. A number of studies have demonstrated unconscious bias toward Asian Americans, including stereotypes about social skills and leadership qualities that can affect hiring and promotion decisions. These studies present identical information to participants about a hypothetical candidate or employee (e.g., educational and work background, expertise, interactions with colleagues), but vary the fictitious person's race. The results suggest that Asian Americans tend to be perceived as competent and technically skilled, but not as leaders.[4] A more recent line of research indicates that Asian Americans also perceive *themselves* as "less prototypical leaders," which translates into lower leadership aspirations—in other words, an internalization of this bias.[5]

Another approach, taken by business or corporate consultants or advisors, points to Asian Americans' "under-developed leadership skills" related to "traditional Asian cultural values such as deference to authority, preference for social harmony/conflict avoidance, and conformance to social norms, among others."[6] These analyses focus on ways that Asian Americans' "background" and "traditional" upbringing yield counterproductive behaviors in the workplace that can be altered with appropriate coaching and mentoring. One popular account in this vein emphasizes the enduring supposed "Confucian values" that underlie Asian American (under)performance at work. We should, however, tread carefully when making such declarations about the "traditional values" of Asian Americans, especially in light of the racialization of Asian Americans as perpetual foreigners, and of Asian /American cultures as backwards and unchanging. We can consider this construction as the flip side of the model minority myth, an oversimplification that fails to take into account the heterogeneity of Asian Americans and the nuances of culture. This essentialist approach reinforces the stereotypes that provide the content for unconscious bias. Labeling Asian Americans' leadership skills as "under-developed" also leaves out the question about whose cultural norms are being used to assess these skills. Can't there be multiple ways to be a good leader across a variety of cultural norms?

A parallel but subtler and more sensitive approach to this "traditional values" take is one that uses empirical evidence (e.g., extensive interviews) to understand real cultural differences, while not essentializing or universalizing Asian American cultures.[7] This research documents the lived experience of Asian Americans who encounter cultural alienation at work. Rather than bemoaning the supposedly sorry state of Asian Americans' leadership skills, this approach points to personal and interpersonal strengths that constitute alternate styles of leadership and that often are not recognized as such. It questions an organizational framework in which Asian Americans are evaluated according to middle-class, Caucasian American cultural standards.[8]

To me, the most powerful and complete way of understanding inequities for Asian Americans and all people of color in the realm of workplace leadership is to realize that organizations themselves are racialized. Models of leadership in any particular context, and the "ideal" behavior that is rewarded in an organization, are informed by and indeed structured by systems of power, such as gender and race. This approach acknowledges the "powerful negative impact of irrational prejudices on socially marginalized groups," but also "underscore[s] the importance of appreciating the institutional (rather than individual) production and reproduction of marginality in organizations and the broader society." Marginality is generated and enforced by "institutional patterns, including organizational rules, procedures, customs, habits, expectations, and images that may not appear to be overtly discriminatory."[9] In other words, an organization's very culture and politics are defined by racialized ideals, which typically will leave people of color at a disadvantage.

The Messiness of Racial and Ethnic Identity

Where I fit into this framework of Asian Americans and leadership is not a straightforward matter. Although I identify strongly as Asian American, I also identify as mixed-race, hapa, mestiza, Filipina American, and, yes, also as white. I realize that I benefit greatly from white privilege; I'm rarely asked those classic questions that set mixed-race people's and Asian Americans' teeth on edge ("What are you?" and "Where are you from?"). My Anglo surname also partially obscures my racial identity. To make matters more confusing, Filipino Americans have a situation unique among Asian Americans, with identities that are shaped by both Spanish and American imperialism. As Professor Anthony Ocampo of Cal Poly Pomona argues, Filipino Americans blur the racial and ethnic lines between Asian Americans and Latinos.[10] The one clear thing in this set of ambiguities is that my racial identity can't be neatly categorized. But even though the lines of my identity tend to shift and blur, I've experienced disaffection and disadvantage along racial and cultural lines in school and work settings, and these scholarly accounts of Asian Americans as "hidden" or "invisible" leaders resonate with me strongly.

The Need for Strategies

As librarians of color, many of us have either personally felt or witnessed in colleagues the effects of everyday racism. All too often, we can tune out or act out as a result of the frustration and isolation of being one of a handful or people of color in a predominantly white workplace. When a significant amount of your time and energy is spent understanding and navigating workplace culture and politics, it can be hard to summon more time and energy to grow as a leader. But our perspectives must move out of the margins. Our libraries need to hear our voices to become stronger, smarter, more relevant, and, dare I say, sites of greater fairness and justice.

Reflecting on my career thus far, I can identify several strategies (some, admittedly, more accidental than intentional) that I used to stay in touch with the reasons I became a librarian and to maintain my commitment to making a difference even when less than ideally situated for impact in my organization.

Making Choices and Taking Action

The following sections represent practical choices and actions I've taken, starting from early days as a librarian, that have put me in a position to engage my motivation to lead. They are ways to develop and practice leadership skills even without an official leadership position in your library. Though perhaps not earth-shattering insights, I hope they offer a few useful and concrete approaches.

Go Where You Have to Go

As a librarian of color, you might not find the leadership opportunities you'd hoped for falling into your lap. Perhaps your organization's definition of "leadership" doesn't match your own understanding of it or your own way of practicing it. Or maybe the leadership opportunities presented to you don't reflect your values, priorities, or interests. Going outside of your organization to work with a professional or community association is an excellent way to create change in an area that truly matters to you.

In my second year as a librarian, I began the first of two terms as the secretary of the Asian Pacific American Librarians Association (APALA) and then served three years as the vice president, president, and immediate past president. APALA, which was founded in 1980, is an association designed to address the needs of Asian Pacific American librarians and those who serve Asian Pacific American communities. My years of service to APALA were formative experiences to me as a new leader. It's no coincidence that this early foray took place in an organization devoted to diversity, one of my passions, and where I worked with colleagues with whom I had cultural experiences in common. APALA gave me a safe space away from obstacles that can be so difficult to navigate for a new librarian of color in a predominantly white organization and where my Asian American identity was a source of community rather than a mark of difference.

As my active involvement in the leadership of APALA wound down, I became more involved with the RUSA History Section, an organization for librarians, archivists, genealogists, and others who work with historical collections and provide research services with historical materials. The History Section gave me the opportunity to collaborate with colleagues with similar professional challenges and interests. We're able to work together to tackle big problems that we all face as history librarians, problems that we cannot address on our own as individual subject specialist librarians.

I have also been involved in initiatives outside the Libraries on the MIT campus. In two stints between 2006 and 2010, I served as the Libraries' representative to the MIT-wide Council on Staff Diversity and Inclusion (CSDI). Because of my work on CSDI, I was recruited to join the Employee Resource Group (ERG) Discovery Team, a group of five staff members from across the Institute brought together to explore the possibility of introducing employee resource groups (ERGs) to MIT. ERGs are employee groups organized around members' shared characteristics, experiences, or interests that provide support and promote career development. After the Discovery Team successfully delivered its recommendations to the Vice President for Human Resources, I then volunteered with a fellow member of the Discovery Team to be the founding co-lead of the Asian Pacific American Employee Resource Group (APA ERG). My experience with APALA was absolutely essential to my leadership of APA ERG, and we established a robust leadership structure, initiated a steady calendar of events, and developed high-level goals for the direction of the ERG. I'm proud to say that the co-leads of the four MIT Employee Resource Groups won the 2014 MIT Excellence Award for Advancing Inclusion and Global Perspectives. This award is a pretty big deal for MIT staff, and it gave us tremendous satisfaction to receive this recognition. It gave me even more satisfaction to develop a thriving campus organization and to find, across MIT, friends, colleagues, and allies in advancing diversity and inclusion.

I'm certain that, like me, you also have many professional issues and concerns that are important to you. Most likely, there's an organization out there that matches your interests and where you can have great impact. If there isn't one, you might be able to find a way to start one. The beauty of this approach to leadership is that you get to plan and execute a vision and make something positive and concrete happen even if you don't have a position of authority in your own workplace.

Develop Your Leadership and Build Your Network

This point might seem obvious, but librarians of color can benefit immensely from opportunities for leadership training and development. As we've seen, the qualities considered to be "ideal" in a leader in many organizations are often more closely aligned with Caucasian Americans' cultural norms and experiences than those of people of color. Leadership development programs give you the opportunity to learn and try out new mind sets, behaviors, and skills. To be clear, I'm not talking about training to better conform to white cultural norms; rather, I see these programs as opportunities to expand your repertoire. If you're fortunate, you'll find a training program that offers the opportunity for a formal self-assessment.

One of the most valuable components of ARL LCDP was the 360-degree assessment tool. Our 2011–12 cohort used the Kouzes and Posner Leadership Practices Inventory, which provides insight into how you see yourself and how others see you as a leader, according to a set of thirty "practices of exemplary leaders." The 360-degree assessment helped me get in better touch with my strengths, and it opened my eyes to areas where I had been falling short or where there was a disconnect between my self-perception and colleagues' perceptions. To be honest, this was an exceedingly uncomfortable experience, forcing very specific self-reflection and presenting me with frank and humbling observations from colleagues. But it's not an exaggeration to call it transformational, and I'm grateful that it showed me concrete areas to focus on my self-development.

Isolation is one of the biggest challenges for librarians of color, and it's an experience that can sap energy and motivation. The opportunity to build a network of friends and colleagues at other institutions is as important a benefit of leadership programs as self-reflection and skill development. If you're able to attend a leadership development program for "underrepresented minorities," it gives you immediate access to highly capable, motivated colleagues who can relate to each other as professionals of color. In addition to ARL LCDP, I've had the good fortune to participate in the ALA Spectrum Institute and the Minnesota Institute in 2004. At all three programs, I've met friends and allies, and all three times, I've been re-energized in my commitment to the profession. The spirit of such smart, energetic, and opinionated people can be infectious. Another key aspect is the periodic emotional sustenance these programs offer. I found it to be liberating and invigorating to have honest and frank conversations with a whole room of people with parallel experiences to mine.

Lead from Where You Are

You don't need an official title to be a leader in organization. Even if you're not the chair of a committee or the head of a department, you can give voice to a perspective that fundamentally influences the group's direction or propose an idea that takes off. To take an example from my own experience, as a member of the MIT Libraries' Committee for the Promotion of Diversity and Inclusion (CPDI), I advocated for the group to move beyond programming, the most typical function of diversity committees. A key example of this was my effort to organize the committee to become actively involved in MIT's search for a new Director of Libraries in 2014. This work included drafting a statement of expectations that we shared with the search committee, which led to an invitation to CPDI for lunch meetings with all four candidates. I then organized the group's preparation for the interviews, as well as a thorough evaluation of the candidates based on the criteria we had set forth, which we again shared with the search committee.

The process the provost used to select the director was complex and mysterious to those of us on the ground, and, keeping perspective on the entire process, I can't imagine that our committee's feedback was at the forefront of his mind as he weighed the options. Still, I believe that our committee's work was an important part of the official feedback from Libraries staff, and it played some role in the eventual selection of our new director. Moreover, it demonstrated to the rest of the Libraries that the committee was prepared to step up to ask necessary but difficult questions and offer our crucial perspectives. It also showed that we could participate proactively in an activity of tremendous consequence for the organization and use our status as an official committee to have influence in an Institute process.

I was a member of CPDI for five years (and rotated off only because of term limits), but I never served as co-chair. Even without official authority, you can tap into your impulse to lead by applying passion, insight, and innovative thinking in any group or setting.

Mind Set and Motivation

The next sections reflect internal characteristics, including some aspects of my basic outlook and temperament that have helped me remain motivated over the years.

Do It for Your Friends

Many of the librarians and archivists of color I've known spend a lot of time discussing workplace politics and dynamics. We debrief, strategize, encourage, seek advice, show newer colleagues the ropes, and sometimes we just vent. This extra work—a form of what has been called the "cultural taxation" of people of color working in higher education—is a necessary form of mutual support by and for people of color.[11] It can also be seen as a form of labor that helps people of color build social capital, the networks of relationships that provide group members with resources and potential benefit. Management scholars have demonstrated that racial similarity is a social capital resource that facilitates "information exchange, social support, and career advancement." In contrast, racial difference can "impede relationship formation and, consequently... limit the organizational benefits resulting from those relationships."[12]

Whether we think of it as building our social capital or as just doing right by our friends and colleagues, many of us have both done this work and benefited from it. You might see something standing in the way of colleagues of color at your own department or library, in the larger organization, or in the profession. I've often found that this provides me with plenty of motivation to try to influence the situation, with interventions either with the colleague of color or with others who might not fully understand that colleague's situation. You might put in a good word about a colleague to help that person get an assignment to an interesting project or task force or try to smooth over a disagreement between colleagues. It might even give you an idea for programs or initiatives at your library, such as the training sessions and discussions we've had at the MIT Libraries about microaggressions and other microcommunications and about implicit bias.

I consider alliances with colleagues of color to be another way of leading from where you are. They are certainly a needed corrective to the unconscious biases that can affect perceptions of and interactions with people of color on the job. Lending an ear to friends or colleagues to help get them back on track is an important service and has a tangible positive impact on the diversity of librarianship.

Embrace Your Values

I opened this chapter by recounting some of the many signs I missed over the years before I came to the library profession. One that I haven't yet mentioned is my long-standing idealistic streak. You won't find many of us who were attracted to librarianship for money and status. Librarianship's core values of access, democracy, diversity, social responsibility, and commitment to the public good resonate profoundly with me and many other library workers. These values are among the main reasons I got into librarianship in the first place.

My ability to stay in touch with these essential values has helped me persist in the profession and provided the motivation for many of my leadership activities, including my work with APALA, the MIT Libraries Committee for the Promotion of Diversity and Inclusion, and the MIT Employee Resource Groups. When you get right down to it, I believe that the work we do every day is of vital importance. Whether buying new books or primary sources that might completely change a student's view of history and society, explaining to a student how to think critically about information, or finding an obscure source for a professor's research on the history or culture of marginalized people, this work is incredibly meaningful to me. I think I perform an essential educational service at MIT, as we all do at our respective institutions. As David A. Thomas and John J. Gabarro pointed out, "intrinsic motivation"—or, as they put it, "loving the work"—is an essential aspect of job satisfaction and persistence.[13]

Keeping your values close can help you see possibilities. It might even give you the optimism you need to try to make a change. And keep in mind that anytime you witness an injustice, it might create another instance of disappointment and frustration, but it can also be an opportunity for leadership.

Take the Long View

The frustrations that librarians of color face can wear on your patience and calm. You might immediately want to right the wrong, or you might struggle with the temptation of speaking or acting out in anger, which is more often than not a counterproductive response. The entrenched aspects of organizational culture that disadvantage people of color can be really quite daunting. What can one person do to improve these situations?

You can't do it alone, and you can't get it all done right now, but you can contribute to achieving some progress. It's been very important to me to take the long view of things. Any goal, of course, has to be reached step by step. I try to assess what can be pragmatically achieved at any moment, and then aim for realistic progress.

My work with CPDI is a good illustration of this approach. I have a number of like-minded colleagues whose values and priorities are a great match with CPDI's work, but who did not want to join the committee in early days because they couldn't imagine it being active, effective, or meaningful enough to be satisfying. For some time, there was some truth to that assessment. We needed to start by focusing on fairly safe programming and to pay close attention to administrative expectations of our work. But as we began to build trust and credibility, our committee was able to grow considerably.

For instance, in 2012, CPDI recommended that the MIT Libraries use ClimateQUAL, the climate assessment tool offered by ARL. After our recommendation was accepted, we were then charged with recruiting our coworkers' participation in the survey. The ClimateQUAL instrument was admittedly imperfect, but it yielded an important result: our report revealed disparities in the perception of climate between employees of color and LGBT employees compared with the employees from majority groups. This finding and other results gave us a solid basis to pursue difficult conversations across the Libraries and in our departments and also formed the basis for CPDI's official statement to the search committee for Director of Libraries.

Another example of the evolution of the committee's role is our participation in an important Institute-wide inclusion initiative. In 2013, MIT President Rafael Reif created a new MIT Institute Community and Equity Office (ICEO) and appointed as its head Professor Ed Bertschinger, a former head of the Physics Department who made great strides in improving the diversity of the Physics graduate program. In early 2015, Ed released a 132-page report outlining a strategic plan to advance a more respectful and inclusive community at MIT. In response to this report, our new director, Chris Bourg, charged CPDI with facilitating group discussions among library staff to gather reactions and feedback. These discussions provided the content for a formal group response from the Libraries to the ICEO. The Libraries have been an exemplar at MIT in engaging with the report in a formal and serious way.

The progress we have made with CPDI was made very clear to me recently in an e-mail from one of the newest members of the committee, a colleague who has been working at the MIT Libraries for less than two years. She had recently attended an Institute-wide lunch discussion on "vulnerability" sponsored by the ICEO, and she said that the subject of CPDI kept coming up during her table's discussion. As their conversation unfolded, she realized that CPDI has served as a bulwark against many of the potential vulnerabilities that library staff might face. According to my colleague, facing these vulnerabilities "can feel less challenging within the Libraries—because we have CPDI on our side." She went on to say, "the Libraries stand out from much of the institute, in that we have this diversity-focused committee that is so influential within the Library community, is so supported by leadership, and has achieved considerable progress." She also perceived that employees in other departments "sorely feel the lack of support and resources that CPDI provides," and that "every department should have a CPDI!" She concluded by asking about the history of our committee: "[W]hat was it like in the MIT Libraries when CPDI was founded? What was the motivation for the founding? How did the group become so integrated into library culture, and influential over time?"

I was amazed to hear this appreciation from a young colleague, and heartened to reflect on the growth we have experienced in the MIT Libraries since the committee's founding more than five years ago. I was present at the creation, and was sometimes frustrated in the early days because I wished we could speak louder, do more, and effect more change. With the leadership of the co-chairs of the group as well as active members like me, we have reached a point where our newest colleagues have not known a workplace where diversity and inclusion aren't central priorities.

Paradigm Shifts

The last sections represent some radical rethinking I've done in recent years, including profound shifts in my thought about both internal and very large-scale external factors that affect my ability to serve as a leader.

Mindfulness

Impatience, anxiety, and anger are all emotional danger zones for people of color in the workplace. I've recommended that you "embrace your values" and "take the long view," but all it takes is one bad interaction, one unfair experience, or one casual and unintended slight to disrupt your focus and cloud your thinking. Reactivity can throw you off balance and undermine your credibility. And as we know, preoccupation and anger can sap your creativity and productivity. How can you see the long view or remember your values when your emotional and mental reactions get in the way?

I can't yet say that I've walked all that far down the path of wisdom, but even as a novice to the practice, I can attest to the power of mindfulness in working with these difficult emotions. Mindfulness is all the rage now, making it into the pages of *Time Magazine*, *The New Yorker*, and even the *Harvard Business Review*. But the principles of mindfulness stretch back thousands of years, deriving from Buddhist philosophies and practices. Although I remain steadfastly secular, I've found these practices to be transformational.[14]

I have the great fortune of living and working near the Cambridge Insight Meditation Center (CIMC), which introduces the practices of *vipassana* and *metta* meditation to hundreds of people a year. CIMC's practice groups and retreats have helped me cultivate greater calm, resilience, trust, and compassion for myself and others. Emotional intelligence is considered an indispensable quality of effective leaders, and no amount of reading or discussion about emotional intelligence can replace the real-life training you'll get from mindfulness practice. As librarians of color, we understand the mistrust, self-doubt, anger, and resignation that can result from institutional racism. Mindfulness practice can help you let go of many of the destructive emotions and reactions that arise from dealing with everyday racism.[15]

One of the key concepts of this practice is non-judgment. Not only is it unnecessary to judge yourself for your mistakes or shortcomings, but it's also not helpful to judge and condemn others for theirs—even when you feel hurt or demeaned by their behavior. A favorite phrase I've learned from programs and practice groups at CIMC is "letting go" of anxiety, anger, vindictiveness, or any other harmful emotion. As I've come to understand it, I can waste my time and energy grinding an axe, or I can let go of my irritation and do something productive. "Letting go" doesn't mean forgetting about injustice. It means stopping your mind from spinning so you can see an injustice clearly. When you can see an entire situation clearly and broadly (i.e., beyond yourself and your bad feelings), you can do something effective rather than reacting based on emotion. It might even make it easier for you to "take the long view."[16]

Another terrific phrase I picked up from CIMC is to "drop your storyline." We can define ourselves by the stories we tell ourselves about our personalities, our abilities, and our potential, or we can drop the stories and just be, and then see what happens. We can assume we know the story behind someone else's actions and behavior, or assume we can't really know. This might lead us to finding out more about what's *really* going on rather than behaving impulsively on a possibly incorrect assumption. A related notion is that every moment is a new moment, and we don't need to be defined by the past. We can tell ourselves stories that calcify self-image and limit possibilities, or we can recognize that in every new moment is an opportunity to take risks, amend our behavior, or see things a new way. Likewise, we don't need to be defined by others' perceptions—we don't need to let anyone else's stories provide our self-definition.[17]

After taking classes focused on mindfulness or *vipassana* meditation, I then attended classes focused on lovingkindness or *metta* meditation. From these practice groups, I understood that acting out of compassion (rather than judgment or anger) is not only the right thing to do, it usually will lead to the best resolution to a difficult situation. A favorite phrase I learned from my *metta* classes is "not making trouble." By "making trouble," I think of actions that spread anger, hurt others back when they hurt you, or just generally make mischief. To be clear, I see this as quite different from being a "troublemaker," as you might find yourself labeled if you speak out or take action about something you think is wrong or unfair. "Making trouble" isn't about making waves, it's about causing needless suffering for yourself and others.[18]

These notions of "letting go," "not making trouble," compassion, and non-judgment might seem like weakness or passivity. On the contrary, I've come to understand anger as weakness, a time that you have diminished agency and are buffeted by emotion. This seems clearest to me when considering some of the greatest leaders against injustice, such as Gandhi, King, and Mandela. The scale of injustice and personal threat that they faced are almost unimaginable to most of us, but they managed to lead with love, peace, and compassion rather than anger and vengeance.

My experience with mindfulness has helped me to truly understand that real change is possible in myself, in others, and in an organization. It has made me more aware of my patterns of behavior and reaction, while at the same time helped me be less hard on myself when I fall back into the more harmful patterns. To many, meditation has mystical or "new-age" connotations, but I have found it to provide the most pragmatic and useful guidance possible.

Two Things to Know: Your Organization Is Structured by Race, and You're Okay

I'd like to turn back to the overview I set out earlier about some of the research that tries to account for the underrepresentation of Asian Americans in leadership across employment sectors. As I've already mentioned, I think that among these possible explanations, the concept of the racialized organization provides the greatest explanatory power. The workplace exists in a larger context of structural inequalities and cultural representations that have been around for centuries, if not longer. These larger structures and forces inform our biases and behaviors, which will inevitably be shaped by race and racism.

As I read those accounts from the scholarly and professional literature, I found that the methodological or philosophical approach primed different types of questions about the challenges for some Asian American leaders. What is this problem about? Is it a problem with me? Do I have to be trained out of supposedly counterproductive "Asian American" behaviors? Is it a problem with coworkers and managers, who need to be trained out of their stereotypes? Or is it also something bigger?

I do agree that leadership development training for people of color is necessary and beneficial, as is cultural competency and diversity awareness training for all employees. Yet I find this to be insufficient. Thinking about these issues at the level of individuals will get us only so far. At some point, we have to understand the necessity of creating cultures of inclusion and equity in our organizations, as well as structures that tend towards dismantling power imbalances rather than reinforcing them.

These are pretty large-scale changes I'm suggesting, and it's hard to imagine where even to start as one person, and perhaps someone without a lot of authority to begin with. So how to take this idea on as an individual? I'd like to suggest that as librarians of color, we should reframe our understanding of leadership. We need to believe that our strengths *are* also leadership.

For example, I have in the past been criticized at work for not speaking up enough in meetings, and I've talked to other Asian American women who have had the same experience. Colleagues can construe quietness as passivity or as withdrawal from the group. But you can also reframe the way you think of this behavior. Taking the time to think through your ideas and providing thoughtful reflection rather than filling the air with talk can be a form of leadership. On the other side of the coin, people of color are also often accused of being "confrontational" or "angry," and this can be interpreted as disruptive or counterproductive behavior. I would argue that a forthright and outspoken assertion—including those uttered with an understandable level of emotion—can be leadership, and indeed might be just the intervention that's called for in a particular situation.

Understanding that an organization is racialized can help to depersonalize interactions where negative attention is called to your difference. It's not so much about personal flaws and shortcomings as it is about existing and persisting in an organization that's shaped by race, with institutional forces at play. This is not to say that you don't need to find ways to adapt so you can succeed in your work culture, but that adaptation doesn't need to be a self-negation. Earlier in this chapter, I advocated for pursuing leadership development to help "expand your repertoire." Here I really do mean *expand,* and not conform. Although we might find a need to undertake personal development for professional success, we also need to embrace our differences. Our differences are also our strengths, and we should have confidence in those strengths even when the dominant culture tries to tell us otherwise.

I am intrigued by an idea described by Stella M. Nkomo and Marcus M. Stewart, a summary of an argument by Diane Grimes and other scholars about "interrogating whiteness." Nkomo and Stewart suggested that "one way to unmask the racialized nature of organizations is to interrogate whiteness.... Interrogating whiteness in organizations means attending to the discourse, images and actions that institutionalize white privilege and domination." They quoted Grimes describing it as "an activity that involves critical reflection about whiteness and privilege and the implications of living in a race-centered society."[19] What would it mean for us to interrogate whiteness in our libraries? Could we, as people of color, begin to document the specific dynamics and interactions where white privilege is manifested? What would it look like for library leadership to take a good, hard look at these mechanisms, and how might we prepare our organizations for such a difficult undertaking?

As librarians of color, I hope we can employ practical strategies to stay on track to meet our potential as leaders. As we grow and develop as leaders, let's understand and take on these larger forces, and I hope that "interrogating whiteness" might be part of this. Step by step, we can work to build awareness, and perhaps help our organizations do the hard but necessary work of truly living up to our profession's values.

NOTES

1. See Deborah Woo, *Glass Ceilings and Asian Americans* (Walnut Creek, CA: AltaMira Press, 2000). For a more recent but less scholarly (and perhaps more problematic) account, see Jane Hyun, *Breaking the Bamboo Ceiling* (New York: HarperCollins, 2005). On the higher education context, see Audrey Yamagata-Noji, "Leadership Development Program in Higher Education: Asian Pacific American Leaders in Higher Education—An Oxymoron?" in *Lessons in Leadership: Executive Leadership Programs for Advancing Diversity in Higher Education,* ed. David J. León (Amsterdam: Elsevier JAI, 2005), 173–206.
2. "There is only 1 Asian woman executive per every 285 Asian women in these companies, half the average ratio of 1 executive per 118 professional men and

women of all races. For Asian men, the executive ratio also falls below average: 1 per 201 Asian men. White women were much more represented, with 1 executive per 123 white women. As expected, white men, with 1 executive per 87, had the highest executive representation." In Buck Gee, Denise Peck, and Janet Wong, *Hidden in Plain Sight* (New York: The Ascend Foundation, 2015), 6, http://c .ymcdn.com/sites/ascendleadership.site-ym.com/resource/resmgr/Research/ HiddenInPlainSight_Paper_042.pdf.

3.   Lei Lai, "The Model Minority Thesis and Workplace Discrimination of Asian Americans," *Industrial and Organizational Psychology: Perspectives on Science and Practice* 6, no. 1 (March 2013): 94–95.

4.   See Thomas Sy et al., "Leadership Perceptions as a Function of Race-Occupation Fit: The Case of Asian Americans," *Journal of Applied* Psychology 95, no. 5 (September 2010): 902–19; Lei Lai and Linda C. Babcock, "Asian Americans and Workplace Discrimination: The Interplay between Sex of Evaluators and the Perception of Social Skills," *Journal of Organizational Behavior* 34, no. 3 (April 2013): 310–26; and Arpi Festekjian et al., "I See Me the Way You See Me: The Influence of Race on Interpersonal Leadership Perceptions," *Journal of Leadership and Organizational Studies* 21, no. 1 (February 2014): 102–19.

5.   Festekjian et al., "I See Me the Way You See Me," 113.

6.   Gee, *Hidden in Plain Sight,* 15.

7.   See Woo, *Glass Ceilings and Asian Americans,* and Tojo Thatchenkery and Kei Sugiyama, *Making the Invisible Visible* (New York: Palgrave Macmillan, 2011).

8.   Thatchenkery and Sugiyama have identified "collaboration, long-term focus, and rewarding the whole" as three key leadership styles demonstrated by Asian Americans. One aspect of this is that Asian Americans tend to less readily "highlight their individual accomplishments" or call attention to themselves. You'd be amazed at how difficult it was for me to write an entire chapter about myself and how I see things. See Thatchenkery and Sugiyama, *Making the Invisible Visible,* 20–21.

9.   Pushkala Prasad, Caroline D'Abate, and Anshuman Prasad, "Organizational Challenges at the Periphery: Career Issues for the Socially Marginalized," in *Handbook of Career Studies,* ed. Hugh Gunz and Maury Peiperl (Thousand Oaks, CA: Sage, 2007): 181.

10.   Anthony Christian Ocampo, *The Latinos of Asia* (Stanford, CA: Stanford University Press, 2016).

11.   Thanks to Eugenia Beh for bringing the idea of "cultural taxation" to my attention. Tiffany D. Joseph and Laura E. Hirshfield, "'Why Don't You Get Somebody New to Do It?' Race and Cultural Taxation in the Academy," *Ethnic and Racial Studies* 34, no. 1 (2011): 121–41.

12.   Erika Hayes James, "Race-Related Differences in Promotions and Support: Underlying Effects of Human and Social Capital," *Organization Science* 11, no. 5 (September–October 2000): 497.

13.   David A. Thomas and John J. Gabarro, *Breaking Through* (Boston: Harvard Business School Press, 1999): 102–3.

14. For a popular account of the therapeutic benefits of meditation and mindfulness, outlined in the context of scientific research, see Daniel J. Siegel, *Mindsight* (New York: Bantam, 2010).
15. Two excellent guides to mindfulness at work are Sharon Salzburg, *Real Happiness at Work* (New York: Workman, 2014), and Chade-Meng Tan, *Search Inside Yourself* (New York: HarperOne, 2012).
16. See Pema Chödrön, *Taking the Leap* (Boston: Shambhala, 2010).
17. For more on breaking out of your usual stories, see Tara Brach, *Radical Acceptance* (New York: Bantam Dell, 2003).
18. An indispensable book about developing a compassionate heart is Pema Chödrön, *Start Where You Are* (Boston: Shambhala, 1994).
19. Stella M. Nkomo and Marcus M. Stewart, "Diverse Identities in Organizations," in *The Sage Handbook of Organization Studies,* ed. Stewart R. Clegg, Cynthia Hardy, Thomas B. Lawrence, and Walter R. Nord (Thousand Oaks, CA: Sage, 2006): 531.

Bibliography

Brach, Tara. *Radical Acceptance: Accepting Your Life with the Heart of a Buddha.* New York: Bantam Dell, 2003.

Chödrön, Pema. *Start Where You Are: A Guide to Compassionate Living.* Boston: Shambhala, 1994.

Chödrön, Pema. *Taking the Leap: Freeing Ourselves from Old Habits and Fears.* Boston: Shambhala, 2010.

Festekjian, Arpi, Susanna Tram, Carolyn B. Murray, Thomas Sy, and Ho P. Huynh. "I See Me the Way You See Me: The Influence of Race on Interpersonal Leadership Perceptions." *Journal of Leadership and Organizational Studies* 21, no. 1 (February 2014): 102–19.

Gee, Buck, Denise Peck, and Janet Wong. *Hidden in Plain Sight: Asian American Leaders in Silicon Valley.* New York: Ascend Foundation, 2015. http://c.ymcdn .com/sites/ascendleadership.site-ym.com/resource/resmgr/Research/ HiddenInPlainSight_Paper_042.pdf.

Hyun, Jane. *Breaking the Bamboo Ceiling: Career Strategies for Asians.* New York: HarperCollins, 2005.

James, Erika Hayes. "Race-Related Differences in Promotions and Support: Underlying Effects of Human and Social Capital." *Organization Science* 11, no. 5 (September–October 2000): 493–508.

Joseph, Tiffany D., and Laura E. Hirshfield. "'Why Don't You Get Somebody New to Do It?' Race and Cultural Taxation in the Academy." *Ethnic and Racial Studies* 34, no. 1 (2011):121–41.

Lai, Lei. "The Model Minority Thesis and Workplace Discrimination of Asian Americans." *Industrial and Organizational Psychology: Perspectives on Science and Practice* 6, no. 1 (March 2013): 93–96.

Lai, Lei, and Linda C. Babcock. "Asian Americans and Workplace Discrimination: The Interplay between Sex of Evaluators and the Perception of Social Skills." *Journal of Organizational Behavior* 34, no. 3 (April 2013): 310–26.

Nkomo, Stella M., and Marcus M. Stewart. "Diverse Identities in Organizations." In *The Sage Handbook of Organization Studies*. Edited by Stewart R. Clegg, Cynthia Hardy, Thomas B. Lawrence, and Walter R. Nord, 520–40. Thousand Oaks, CA: Sage, 2006.

Ocampo, Anthony Christian. The Latinos of Asia: How Filipino Americans Break the Rules of Race. Stanford, CA: Stanford University Press, 2016.

Prasad, Pushkala, Caroline D'Abate, and Anshuman Prasad. "Organizational Challenges at the Periphery: Career Issues for the Socially Marginalized." In *Handbook of Career Studies*. Edited by Hugh Gunz and Maury Peiperl, 169–87. Thousand Oaks, CA: Sage, 2007.

Salzburg, Sharon. *Real Happiness at Work: Meditations for Accomplishment, Achievement, and Peace*. New York: Workman, 2014.

Siegel, Daniel J. *Mindsight: The New Science of Personal Transformation*. New York: Bantam, 2010.

Sy, Thomas, Lynn M. Shore, Judy Strauss, Ted H. Shore, Susanna Tram, Paul Whiteley, and Kristine Ikeda-Muromachi. "Leadership Perceptions as a Function of Race-Occupation Fit: The Case of Asian Americans." *Journal of Applied Psychology* 95, no. 5 (September 2010): 902–19.

Tan, Chade-Meng. *Search Inside Yourself: The Unexpected Path to Achieving Success, Happiness (and World Peace)*. New York: HarperOne, 2012.

Thatchenkery, Tojo, and Kei Sugiyama. *Making the Invisible Visible: Understanding Leadership Contributions of Asian Minorities in the Workplace*. New York: Palgrave Macmillan, 2011.

Thomas, David A., and John J. Gabarro. *Breaking Through: The Making of Minority Executives in Corporate America*. Boston: Harvard Business School Press, 1999.

Woo, Deborah. *Glass Ceilings and Asian Americans: The New Face of Workplace Barriers*. Walnut Creek, CA: AltaMira Press, 2000.

Yamagata-Noji, Audrey. "Leadership Development Program in Higher Education: Asian Pacific American Leaders in Higher Education—An Oxymoron?" In *Lessons in Leadership: Executive Leadership Programs for Advancing Diversity in Higher Education*. Edited by David J. León, 173–206. Amsterdam: Elsevier JAI, 2005.

Chapter 5

TRYING TO FASHION
A WORLD
Facilitating the Revolution with
Critical Librarianship

Deborah Lilton

For my people standing staring trying to fashion a better way
from confusion, from hypocrisy and misunderstanding,
trying to fashion a world that will hold all the people,
all the faces, all the adams and eves and their countless generations;
                                                    ~Margaret Walker, 1937

TO MY KNOWLEDGE, I am the first African American librarian to work in the Central Library at Vanderbilt University. I am also the first nonwhite librarian to work in the Collection Development Department at this library, which serves as the "main" library on campus. I do not write this from a place of pride but rather from a place of practicality. In a very real sense, my body politic frames everything I do while at work. Often-times there is an assumption embedded in the concept of "being the first" that something about that person is "special." Not special in the generic sense that "we are all special," but actually somehow different from all the others who tried and did not succeed prior to the first. And if you are the first in a particular racial or ethnic category to accomplish some feat, win some award, or attain a level of professional employment, the stakes are a bit higher, especially if you are employed at an organization where most of the janitorial, cafeteria, and ground maintenance staff look like you, yet (surprisingly) you don't hold any of those positions. No matter how you dress or talk or walk, your physical self is always there testifying to the difference that you have—that visible difference that you share with others in more "menial" positions than yourself. So whether you want to be or not, you will be seen as a role model—somehow different from those who look like you, but have yet to acquire the same level of position as you.

In the introduction to a journal issue of *Critical Inquiry* focused on "the complex interplay among race, writing, and difference,"[1] noted literary critic Henry Louis Gates Jr. describes race "as a trope of ultimate, irreducible difference between cultures, linguistic groups, or adherents of specific belief systems."[2] This "trope of difference" is in full play in the arena of academic librarianship. While I would like to have the opportunity to choose to be a "role model" or a "credit to my race," that is not a choice afforded to me. Not out of malice or spite but simply because I am the "first," I am a role model by default. Instead of resenting or lamenting this fact, I have embraced it and learned to use it to my advantage to meet new people, learn new skills, and explore new opportunities.

MEETING NEW PEOPLE

Initially, I was hired as the Librarian for English, Theatre, and Film Studies. My predecessor was employed for over thirty years at this institution—even receiving his PhD in English from Vanderbilt University. Some might say I had large shoes to fill. Luckily, I didn't know these details until after a year or so on the job. By then, I had already begun noticing gaps in the English literature collection as well as the growing interdisciplinary nature of English and literary studies at the university. As my colleagues asked me to share purchases with them, I discovered just how much literature touched almost every humanities discipline and at times even some social science ones too. In addition, having received my MA in English from Rutgers University in 2004, I was emboldened to trust my own judgment and subject expertise training by my first supervisor, Mary Beth Blalock, Head of Collection Development at Central Library, and my mentor, Peter Brush, former Librarian for History, African-American Diaspora Studies, East Asian Studies, and Jewish Studies. In effect, I was modifying my predecessor's collection development policy and broadening the notion of literature beyond canonical works of literature and criticism. The idea of destabilizing the literary canon is best explained by literary theorist Terry Eagleton, in his best-selling work, *Literary Theory: An Introduction*:

> But it does mean that the so-called 'literary canon', the unquestioned 'great tradition' of the 'national literature', has to be recognized as a construct, fashioned by particular people for particular reasons at a certain time. There is no such thing as a literary work or tradition which is valuable in itself, regardless of what anyone might have said or come to say about it. 'Value' is a transitive term: it means whatever is valued by certain people in specific situations, according to particular criteria and in the light of given purposes.[3]

I was fashioning the English literature collection to fit the current student and faculty needs at Vanderbilt University unpinned from static notions of the literary canon. No one questioned my decisions as I ordered more contemporary literary fiction, creative writing guides, and experimental volumes of poetry (to complement the newly formed Creative Writing Program), and a little less literary criticism. I have simultaneously enjoyed the autonomy of collection building in particular disciplines while appreciating the collaborative nature of being a liaison.

I cannot say enough about how helpful it was to have a colleague and mentor like Peter Brush. Musser's article "Effective Retention Strategies for Diverse Employees" highlights the importance of mentoring:

> Mentors help the new employee understand the unwritten rules of the workplace and the cultural/organizational norms. Issues such as the preferred organizational communication style, assertiveness, the importance

of socializing, learning when it is acceptable to refuse
assignments, and creating the balance between work
and home are all important rules that a mentor can help
employees master.[4]

Librarianship was my mentor's second career, and he approached it
with an efficient critical passion that I still aspire to until this very day.
Whenever I felt I was floundering a bit due to all the changes happening
in the library, in my department, and the publishing field, he would re-
mind me that his job remained virtually unchanged his first ten years in
librarianship and that afforded him the opportunity to hone his skills, but
that each year since I started I had to learn something new: a revised pro-
cedure, a new reporting line, a modified fund structure, and so on. Since I
was chasing a moving target, it was best to pace myself and not to get out
of breath. With that insightful nugget, I began truly paying attention to my
surroundings and resisting the urge to compare myself to any of the other
collection development librarians. Without the support of my supervisor
and the encouragement of my mentor, I would have found it difficult to
adapt to the ever-changing environment.

BEING FLEXIBLE OR COMFORTABLE WITH CHANGE

When I slowed down and stopped chasing the moving target, I noticed
that the "graying of the profession" was happening right before my very
eyes. After one year at my job, the head of my library retired. The second year, the head of my department retired. The third year, the head of
the library system retired. The fourth year, a Dean of Libraries was hired.
The sixth year, my mentor, Peter Brush, Vietnam war scholar and history
librarian extraordinaire, retired. The seventh year, the head of reference
retired and the Dean of Libraries retired. I am in the third month of my
eighth year as a professional academic librarian, and I can tell you that
working amid constant change is the name of the game.

Staff changes aside, collection building has changed quite a bit since
I started at Vanderbilt University as well. Approval plans, funding structures, and ordering processes have changed several times over in order to
keep pace with rapid changes in the publishing world. For example, when

I was initially trained in collection development, the tools of the trade were paper announcement slips and customized rubber stamps designating my funds and subject areas. Now, I receive weekly e-mails with links to my electronic notifications.

Coping with change and working in the midst of change is a skill I have mastered over time. During my adolescence and early adulthood, I shied away from change as I believed it signaled insecurity and caused chaos. I have since learned that change is a natural part of life; the more we try to avoid it the more we encounter it. At work, I have learned to deal with change by learning how to manage it and modifying my attitude toward it. Even if my initial reaction is that the change will produce unsavory effects, I consciously delay judgment and look for the positives that this change may bring. I realize that the ways I think about change will affect how I perceive change in my work environment. In "Enhancing Readiness for Change by Enhancing Mindfulness," Gärtner writes:

> These studies have shown the relevance of mindfulness
> for organizations that face changing environments;
> when situations, constellations or information change,
> it is imperative to maintain an attention on external and
> internal stimuli in order to establish a more nuanced
> appreciation of the situation and be prepared to man-
> age complex and conflicting issues, as well as negative
> affective arousal.[5]

While the stereotype of librarians revolves around anal-retentive, detail-obsessed behaviors, a more accurate view of twenty-first-century library work involves problem solving and decision making amid high levels of ambiguity in a rapidly changing information landscape connected to an even more rapidly changing publishing industry, all filtered through "a faster than the speed of light" technological invention known as the Internet.

While my mentor, my supervisor, and even my colleagues helped me adapt as a new librarian, refine concrete skills I learned in library school, and even cope with the rapid change in the library landscape, the one thing they could not show me how to do was navigate "the politics of representation" that go along with being "the first African American librarian" at a predominantly white university in the South. This was something that I had to figure out for myself. It is something that every person of color who is "the first" or the "only one" has to navigate. It is a skill acquired over time and with practice. Needless to say, I am still learning even as I type these words.

LEARNING NEW SKILLS

Being an academic librarian requires both concrete and abstract skills. Concrete skills are the ones that we typically learn about in library school—building collections, cataloging materials, conducting a reference interview and the like, while abstract skills are the ones that we learn through experience whether in the classroom, the conference room, or the board room. Emotional intelligence, team building, and managing from the middle—these are just a few I have learned on the job. However, as a minority librarian working at a predominantly white institution (PWI), the most important abstract skill I have learned is how to manage the politics of [racial] representation.

The phrase "the politics of representation" was initially coined by Stuart Hall, a cultural theorist and sociologist of Jamaican descent in his article entitled "New Ethnicities." While the concept is a complex one, I don't plan to use it in a theoretical sense but rather a practical one. Hall describes the politics of representation as "how things are represented and the machineries and regimes of representation in a culture."[6] What this means is that representations draw meaning from the situations within which they reside and don't just reflect meaning of an abstract thing or idea. And this meaning is constructed by each individual viewing said representation, so there is no one true or verifiable meaning but instead a plethora of meanings.

Oftentimes I am asked to complete tasks that are outside of my job description but for which I am deemed a good fit because of my race or ethnicity. Library literature has noted this is a common occurrence for minority librarians entering the field of academic librarianship:

> Faculty of color more frequently find themselves burdened with teaching loads and service responsibilities that may detract from their research activity. ... They are

usually expected to assume institutional roles (such as that of the "diversity specialist") that are often ignored in terms of tenure and promotion evaluations.[7]

For example, I have represented the library at a *Wikipedia* edit-a-thon dedicated to Nashville civil rights during Black History Month. I have been asked to give library tours to "disadvantaged" public school children who attended a local charter school. I have conducted a research skills session at a summer institute for incoming first-generation college students. Finally, I have been asked to curate numerous civil rights exhibits using materials from Vanderbilt Special Collections. While I enjoyed most of the tasks and learned new skills from all of them, I also have felt the strain of being "the role model": Who do I represent? How am I representing them? And to what end? What is the purpose of this representation? These are questions I have asked myself from time to time. In each of these instances, I felt myself juxtaposed against "the innocent notion of the essential black subject."[8]

With each task, I got the opportunity to learn new skills and exposed to various types of patrons that I don't usually work with (elementary and middle school students); however, it must be noted that each task also required time away from my routine duties. Sometimes I had to make up that time by staying later at work and sometimes completing routine tasks from home so as to keep abreast of daily tasks. For me and other academic librarians of color, especially those on the tenure track, the politics of representation at predominantly white colleges and universities usually results in "cultural taxation." Amado M. Padilla coined this term in 1996 while writing about scholars of color in academia who

> frequently find ourselves having to respond to situations
> that are imposed on us by the administration which
> assumes that we are best suited for specific tasks because
> of our race/ethnicity or our presumed knowledge of
> cultural differences.[9]

In order to avoid burnout, I have had to learn how to be strategic with my time as well as manage the effects of cultural taxation on my daily workload. Time is the greatest commodity that any of us have, so learning to focus our time on tasks where we can make the greatest contributions is key. For example a few years ago I was asked to give a presentation on a well-known Nashville civil rights leader at a local conference. While I have working knowledge of this person's life from curating an exhibit on him, I turned down that opportunity because I am not an expert on his life or the Baptist community in Nashville. I did a quick cost-benefit analysis in my mind—my presence alone would not be enough—that is, body politics. This task would require too much effort on my part and time away from my routine duties to be worth the cost. Several projects I am currently working on—including the writing of this chapter—are more important and intrinsically rewarding. Time on the job has taught me this as well as given me the courage to say "NO." Oftentimes the politics of representation cuts both ways—paradoxically both expanding and limiting opportunities for professional growth. Learning how to manage it is a skill that I have acquired over time.

Exploring New Opportunities

In these last few years at my job, I have gotten to explore new opportunities through new roles inside my organization as well outside in the larger library community. This has been an exciting time in my career development as I have been challenged to grow beyond my typical skill set as a liaison librarian. Being trusted with more responsibilities outside of my typical job duties has been a very rewarding experience. Three examples stand out: (1) chairing the system-wide Collection Committee, (2) chairing the Poster Sessions Committee for the 9th National Conference for African American Librarians, and (3) presenting at the 2015 Diversity Summit at the Texas Library Association Conference.

Last year, I began serving on the Collections Committee, and in the middle of the year, I was asked to chair the committee for a two-year term. As the youngest librarian on the committee, I was surprised that I had been asked and not a more senior employee; however, my supervisor saw how proficient I was at training a new librarian as well as creating documentation to go with that training so that he believed I was the right person for the job. The previous chair walked me through the committee procedures as well as previous projects they had completed during her tenure. Now, I am interacting on a regular basis with librarians across the system and helping to make collection decisions in a collaborative environment. Chairing the committee was a medium learning curve for me as I am learning to flex my team-building muscles, to delegate tasks to members with specialized expertise, and to mediate communication between the committee, the other Collection Development Librarians, and the Head of System-wide Collections. I am sure this will be an enriching experience as I continue to learn about collections from a 50,000-foot view.

Last year a colleague whom I had known since library school approached me with an offer to serve on a national conference planning committee as well as chair a subcommittee for the 9th National Conference for African American Librarians (NCAAL). This was an unexpected opportunity, but I rearranged my schedule to make room for this challenge. I was intrinsically motivated to give back to an organization, the Black Caucus of the American Library Association, which has supported me in both big and small ways throughout my career. From their mentoring program to their welcoming attitude to all interested in learning about the profession, I have greatly benefited from being a part of this ethnic caucus since my library school days. Furthermore, I believed the skills and networks I would build from this national committee assignment would outweigh any challenges related to time, technique, and team. My experience was very fruitful. Not only did I get to practice my team-building skills learned from chairing the Collections Committee at my home organization when I had to invite and encourage others to serve on this committee, but I also was exposed to additional facets of conference planning such as disseminating a call for proposals, choosing poster sessions, developing a rubric for presenters, documenting the event with photographs and social media news feed posts, choosing judges, developing a rubric and point system for the judges, announcing award winners, and soliciting feedback after the event from the participants. While I have given a poster session several times, it was my first time being on the other side of the looking glass. It was an eye-opening experience that called upon all my mental and physical resources.

The last example I will offer was the most unexpected of all and perhaps the most challenging as well. In the spring of 2015 I was asked to be one of the speakers at the second annual Diversity Summit at the Texas Library Association's annual conference. I was shocked and a bit frightened—even questioning my own expertise. Who was I to talk about diversity? Why would the audience want to listen to me? However, I was both intrinsically and extrinsically motivated to accept the invitation. Not only did I want to prove to myself that I could rise to the challenge, but for the first time I was being *invited* to speak *based on a previous presentation* I had given at another national conference, ACRL 2013. I was to be a guest of the Texas Library Association and not only a conference participant! My topic was to be one I had presented on before, but this time instead of presenting to a curious audience I was presented to an audience who was hungry to know more, and more than likely had practical tasks at their institutions they wanted to apply my presentation to. My topic was "The Psychological Contract and the Minority Librarian." My presentation was part of a larger panel that discussed factors that were likely affecting the retention of minority librarians while also providing concrete suggestions to reduce the effects of these factors. I was presenting on a topic from organizational management literature although I had never managed a single person, save a work-study student, before. While I was well-versed in the literature, breaking down the concept to those who had never heard about it before was a challenge. I practiced on coworkers, friends, and anyone who would listen. I consulted with a colleague who is a Prezi expert to help me construct a presentation that used an image to make the invisible concept of psychological contract visible.

All three of these unexpected opportunities taught me that I enjoy being challenged and working collaboratively with others. While much of my job consists of routine tasks, the portions of my job where I get to engage in creative thinking and problem solving while analyzing the academic library environmental landscape appeal to me the most. Because the organizational culture at my library is built on professionalism and trust, I have been allowed to explore various avenues of research and service. I greatly appreciate the autonomy and self-direction that my current position has afforded me. In Daniel Pink's *Drive*, autonomy is described as one of the three elements essential to employee motivation:

> A sense of autonomy has a powerful effect on individual performance and attitude. According to a cluster of recent behavioral science studies, autonomous motivation promotes greater conceptual understanding, better grades, enhanced persistence at school and in sporting

activities, higher productivity, less burnout, and greater levels of psychological well-being.[10]

I view the complexities of my tenure as a librarian at a predominantly white university through the lens of critical librarianship. Toni Samek broadly defined it as "an international movement of library and information workers that consider the human condition and human rights above other professional concerns."[11] Nicole Pagowsky gave a more detailed definition; critical librarianship "examines existing power structures, inequality, and rhetoric in society, and how these things get reinforced within…the library as an institution."[12] How does America's relationship to diversity as a concept and minorities as a whole affect or influence my day-to-day experience as an African American librarian who works at a predominantly white university in the South? While I don't consciously think about my ethnicity day in and out, it is always there. For me, everything I do at my job is framed by the fact that I am the first African American librarian in my department and in my branch library. For me, diversity is not just a touchstone, a movement, or a trend, I am the walking, talking embodiment of the concept every day at work. While this is not without its challenges, to be sure, I relish my job and long for the day when the collision of my ethnicity and my choice of profession becomes commonplace.

Amid semester deadlines, comprehensive exams, and senior theses, it is easy to forget what best-selling author and cultural critic Walter Moseley reminded the audience of during his closing plenary at the 9th National Conference for African American Librarians: "Reading is a revolutionary act."[13] My job, as I see it, is to facilitate the revolution. Of course, I am not talking about a revolution propelled by guns or threats of violence but instead a revolution of ideas. I am a descendant of those who were bought and sold on the open market in this country for over 240 years, when a slave discovered reading or writing could be punished by death at the worst and a severe flogging at the least. In a very real sense, then, for African Americans, reading has always preceded the revolution. In fact, this is not true just for African Americans but for all Americans. Consider this: a single man with one pen set the British colonies of the North American continent ablaze with talk of independence at the start of the fateful year of 1776. His fifty-page pamphlet entitled "Common Sense" was read across the nation in the same year that America would declare its independence from Mother Britain. This single document is now seen as one of the major catalysts mobilizing the colonists to begin fighting a bloody eight-year battle that would later be called the American Revolution. This one example demonstrates that while reading is often viewed as a solitary act, its consequences can be far-reaching: molding the shape of history for years to come. It is within this stream of history that I and other librarians stand, identifying, describing, and building collections that we hope will live past our lifetimes and sustain future generations of orators, statesmen, activists, and philosophers.

NOTES

1. Henry Louis Gates Jr., "Editor's Introduction: Writing 'Race' and the Difference It Makes," *Critical Inquiry* 12, no. 1 (Autumn 1985): 15, http://www.jstor.org/stable/1343459.
2. Ibid., 5.
3. Terry Eagleton, *Literary Theory*, 2nd ed. (Hoboken, NJ: Wiley, 2011), 10.
4. Linda R. Musser, "Effective Retention Strategies for Diverse Employees," in *Diversity Now: People, Collections, and Services in Academic Libraries*, ed. Teresa Y. Neely and Kuang-Hwei Lee-Smeltzer (Binghamton, NY: Haworth Press, 2001), 68.
5. Christian Gärtner, "Enhancing Readiness for Change by Enhancing Mindfulness," *Journal of Change Management* 13, no. 1 (2013), 53.
6. Stuart Hall, *Critical Dialogues in Cultural Studies*, ed. David Morely and Kuan-Hsing Chen (New York: Routledge, 1996), 444.
7. Ibid.
8. Ione T. Damasco and Dracine Hodges, "Tenure and Promotion Experiences of Academic Librarians of Color," *College and Research Libraries* 73, no. 3 (May 2012), 282.
9. Amado M. Padilla, "Ethnic Minority Scholars, Research, and Mentoring: Current and Future Issues," *Educational Researcher* 23, no. 4 (May 1994), 26.
10. Daniel H. Pink, *Drive* (New York: Riverhead Books 2009), 88–89.
11. Toni Samek, quoted in Tara, "Critical Librarianship: An Interview with Toni Samek," *The (Unofficial) BCLA Intellectual Freedom Committee Blog*, November 13, 2007, https://bclaifc.wordpress.com/2007/11/13/critical-librarianship-an-interview-with-toni-samek/.
12. Nicole Pagowsky, "Transforming Our Image through a Compass of Critical Librarianship" (keynote address, Wisconsin Association of Academic Librarians, Manitowoc, WI, April 22, 2015), http://nicolepagowsky.info/documents/PagowskyWAAL2015Transcript.pdf.
13. Walter Mosley, "Closing Keynote," (9th National Conference for African American Librarians, Closing Plenary, St. Louis, MO, August 7, 2015).

BIBLIOGRAPHY

Damasco, Ione T., and Dracine Hodges. "Tenure and Promotion Experiences of Academic Librarians of Color." *College and Research Libraries* 73, no. 3 (May 2012): 279–301.

Eagleton, Terry. *Literary Theory: An Introduction*, 2nd ed. Hoboken, NJ: Wiley, 2011.

Gärtner, Christian. "Enhancing Readiness for Change by Enhancing Mindfulness." *Journal of Change Management* 13, no. 1 (2013): 52–68.

Gates, Henry L., Jr. "Editor's Introduction: Writing 'Race' and the Difference It Makes." *Critical Inquiry* 12, no. 1 (Autumn 1985): 1–20. http://www.jstor.org/stable/1343459.

Hall, Stuart. *Critical Dialogues in Cultural Studies*. Edited by David Morely and Kuan-Hsing Chen. New York: Routledge, 1996.

Mosley, Walter. "Closing Keynote." 9th National Conference for African American Librarians, Closing Plenary, St. Louis, MO, August 7, 2015.

Musser, Linda R. "Effective Retention Strategies for Diverse Employees." In *Diversity Now: People, Collections, and Services in Academic Libraries*. Edited by Teresa Y. Neely and Kuang-Hwei Lee-Smeltzer, 63–72. Binghamton, NY: Haworth Press, 2001.

Padilla, Amado M. "Ethnic Minority Scholars, Research, and Mentoring: Current and Future Issues." *Educational Researcher* 23, no. 4 (May 1994): 24–27.

Pagowsky, Nichole. "Transforming Our Image through a Compass of Critical Librarianship," Keynote address, Wisconsin Association of Academic Librarians, Manitowoc, WI, April 22, 2015. http://nicolepagowsky.info/documents/PagowskyWAAL2015Transcript.pdf.

Pink, Daniel H. *Drive: The Surprising Truth about What Motivates Us*. New York: Riverhead Books 2009).

Tara. "Critical Librarianship: An Interview with Toni Samek." *The (Unofficial) BCLA Intellectual Freedom Committee Blog*, November 13, 2007. https://bclaifc.wordpress.com/2007/11/13/critical-librarianship-an-interview-with-toni-samek/.

Chapter 6[*]

OUT OF THE BOX

Meredith R. Evans, PhD

WHEN I WAS asked to write a chapter to share my leadership journey, it did not occur to me that when I sat down to write, I would have to give new, serious thought to my stance on leadership as a whole and my relationship to leadership in particular. Today, one never has to scroll far into their LinkedIn feed to find countless blog posts, inspirational quotes, and cautionary tales on the woes of "bad" leadership. Gems like "Managers are all about the bottom line while leaders see the big picture" or Drucker's famous "Management is doing things right; leadership is doing the right things"[1] forced me to really consider where my own style fit into all of this. What I settled on was that my journey and my successes have been situational, as described in the theoretical framework Motivation to Lead and informed by *The 7 Habits of Highly Effective People.*[2]

The Motivation to Lead framework attempts to understand how one develops as a leader and how one's different, individual behaviors factor into that development. It takes into consideration cognitive ability, values, personality, and attitudes. The authors conclude that there are three ways in which individuals decide to lead: (1) Affective—those who enjoy leading; (2) Social normative—those who feel it is their duty to lead, and (3) Non-calculative—those who do not consider the sacrifice or risk of leading. The studies that use Motivation to Lead mostly conclude that a person's desire to lead is situational and can be influenced by the work, the team, or the achievement. The truth is, leadership and management go hand in hand and both have a rightful place in creating successful organizations. The difference between the two is that leaders have people who follow them, while managers have people who work for them. For some, leadership is an innate and intuitive characteristic; for others, it is a learned skill, but any type of leader must acknowledge that success is foremost about balancing the tactical (management) and vision (leadership).

My motivation to lead is non-calculative; "I don't expect to get any privileges if I agree to lead or be responsible for a project."[3] Perhaps my motivation to excel is social normative, a commitment to changing societal norms and a desire to help others succeed. Conversely, my ability to manage comes from many years of formal and informal training, including some formative years working in the food and hospitality industry. I have read countless books and articles on this topic, and although they have not always supported my opinion, it is my firm belief that managing goes beyond approving vacation requests and assigning tasks. Many managers succeed despite the "benefits" of executive exposure or support; successful ones learn how to nurture and leverage relationships, rely on front-line trends to predict the future, and engender deep trust amongst their teams.

From working in pizza joints to leading in libraries, my career has been ambitious, rewarding, and somewhat quirky. I look back today and see that my journey may seem disjointed to many, but I am clear that each experience prepared me for the next opportunity. Despite personal tragedy; harsh words from professors, colleagues, and bosses; and other challenging situations along the way, I have crafted a career that includes deep and meaningful learning experiences and successfully held increasingly high-level positions in librarianship. I questioned myself and others along the way, but my career flourished when I learned to balance outside assumptions and personal authenticity.

For years I thought of myself in layers—as a New Yorker, as an African American, as a woman, as an African American woman, and later as an archivist, a librarian, a scholar, a manager, and a mother. The more seasoned I become, the more layers apply and the more faceted the lens through which I view the world becomes. My journey has been full of psychological and personality tests, self-awareness assessments, and leadership trainings. From Myers-Briggs Type Indicators to 360-degree assessments, I used these tools to develop a management style that is more amenable to the library and academic culture. With the enjoyment of being middle-aged, my leadership style, combined with corporate experience, education, and faith, I am the first African American female director of a Presidential Library. Here is my story.

THE HELPFUL DETOUR

Surrounded by male coworkers who referred to women only in demeaning ways, I chose to be called "Queen" to ensure a level of respect or difference. "Thank you for calling _____ Pizza; would you like to try a special?" Four hours a night, four nights a week for my last two years of college, this is how I answered the phone—except the one night my sister and family friend walked through the door. At that moment I could no longer speak: I knew she had come to tell me that my father had passed.

A few months later I graduated from college with a degree in history, and while waiting for graduate school acceptance letters, I switched to full-time at the pizza shop. Almost a year passed, as did all of my grad school acceptance deadlines. Both my parents held positions in larger corporations; my mother, in her corporate way, felt moved to call and in mid-conversation said, "Is this place a job or a career?" Those words changed my life. In hindsight, I now know that what would happen next is Habit 1 of *The 7 Habits of Highly Effective People*: "Be proactive."[4] I took those words to heart and though I didn't rush back into graduate school, by age 25 I was supervising seven pizza stores in Detroit, Michigan, grossing over three million dollars in sales a year cumulatively—and taking home close to six figures myself. My foray into professional and corporate life exposed me to training that enhanced my natural leadership skills and informs my management style even today. The most memorable was Situational Leadership.[5] Situational Leadership theory and training was developed by Paul Hersey and Ken Blanchard[6] and challenges leaders to apply "task-relevant" solutions when determining how best to meet goals and manage people. Situational leaders learn how to effectively influence people to accomplish goals based on the unique circumstances at hand, as opposed to a standard approach applied to any problem or situation. The four competencies are Diagnose: "Understand the situation they are trying to influence"; Adapt: "Adjust their behavior in response to the contingencies of the situation"; Communicate: "Interact with others in a manner they can understand and accept"; Advance: "Manage the movement."[7] As a young, high-performing Area Supervisor, certified in Situational Leadership and inspired by Blanchard's *One Minute Manager*,[8] I was able to improve team morale and repeatedly produce tangible results.

However, ten years in the food and hospitality industry began to take its toll. Sexism only slightly outweighed racism, the lack of racial and gender diversity became more of a deterrent, and meaningful changes seemed nonexistent. Sometimes things were subtle and other times they were blatant. Few women were in top-level positions, and managers of color were often limited to specific demographic areas that often had higher crime rates. Meetings were also often held at locations completely insensitive to gender dynamics, such as strip clubs or water parks. Coping with societal challenges like systemic racism and sexism motivated me to climb the corporate ladder.

With the *Minority Executives' Handbook* by my side[9] and a few mentors to converse with, I learned how to navigate the waters and secure my seat at the executive table. Through it all I turned stores around, increasing profits while establishing each store as a desirable and vital part of each community. I watched staff members with GEDs become store managers and pizza delivery drivers open their own franchises. Lives were changing, and I felt honored to contribute to an experience that I had learned so much from.

Though retail management and food service were not my original plan after college, I have no regrets and will continue to tell anyone, "Walk through the door when it opens and do not overthink it." The skills I gained from my first career have benefited me greatly in my current one. In hindsight, I may have been running from the grief of losing a parent, but the truth is it was much easier for me to work and focus on the success that was within my reach than to figure out financial aid and graduate school like my friends did. While they were in master's and PhD programs or getting married, I had become a homeowner and was steadily moving up the corporate ladder. Timing is everything and rarely what you expect. My friends and I would all go on to accomplish similar things in due time; my story would simply include a few chapters theirs did not.

COURSE CORRECTION...ALMOST

After falling asleep at the table one Christmas dinner, I realized my life had to change. I realized that I had allowed a great tragedy in my college years to create a detour that took me far from my original career trajectory—graduate school, a doctorate, and then historian/university faculty member. I had failed to implement Covey's Habit 2, "Begin with the end in mind,"[10] but I was ready to get back on track. I took a more flexible job waiting tables and applied for graduate school.

After much consultation I chose library science. The path to becoming a historian seemed daunting and restrictive, and I didn't want to risk being a protégé for seven to nine years under someone who did not think like me or look like me or see the world like I did. I had friends from my undergraduate years who had become librarians, and after speaking with several of them I knew that my heart was with not simply history, but specifically with the material that served the writing of history. Inspired by my memories of meeting Nelson Mandela, C. Eric Lincoln, John Hope Franklin, Nell Painter, and Evelyn Brooks Higginbotham, to name a few, and my research as a United Negro College Fund (UNCF) Mellon fellow, the path into library science became clearer. I also knew this choice could lead to a management position that would allow me to be home before the sun went down.

In search of quality of life, I left the industry that had kept me working six and a half days a week. I walked away from a great salary and an awesome team and enrolled at my alma mater, Clark Atlanta University. I knew I could recharge by being in a familiar place that had a legacy of strong and successful African American alumni in the profession. I picked up a minimum wage job in a local archive and a roommate to help defray the cost of my mortgage and began studying to become not a librarian, but actually an archivist (remember, I had begun my academic journey as a historian).

Unfortunately my matriculation collided with the library school's dwindling finances and struggles to remain open. While assisting with the accreditation process, my path shifted, and for the first time in years I considered a doctorate so that I could teach at my alma mater.

"Scared of Me"

Many decisions in my life have been practical, and I realize now that some were the result of feeling pressured to be genteel or a result of the confidence I exude when expressing my beliefs and ideas. As I developed as a leader, I often struggled with how to reconcile my skill set, my management style, and my personal identity to ensure I was presenting an authentic version of myself to the world. I am reminded of Covey's 7 *Habits*, specifically Habit 5 "Seek first to understand, then to be understood," and Habit 6, "Synergize."[11] These are two competencies that require people to embrace diversity, not resist it. Scholars continue to write about the struggles with issues related to race, ethnicity, gender identity, religion, language, and culture. It is often stated that "despite increasing explicit pronouncements of tolerance for diversity, actual accounts of work place discrimination are on the rise."[12]

I believe many people of color just want to be respected for their skill set, knowledge, and experience, without the added burden of being assumed to be a subject matter or cultural expert on race. This felt especially hard as a person of color who was not well represented in her chosen field of study. My student and professional careers have been a mix of consistent brushes with implicit bias, with occasional racial or gender-related microaggressions thrown in for good measure.

These are not new psychological theories. They are subtle behaviors or prejudices in action. Be they many or few, all of these experiences have been learning lessons for how I would craft my career and how I would interact with my peers and my teams along the way. Upon completion of my master's degree, I chose between a library residency program in California and pursuing a doctorate in library science in North Carolina. I initially wanted to master the full range of my newfound skills in librarianship before teaching, but the cards fell on the side of the doctorate instead. As much as I wanted a higher salary and to live more comfortably again, I followed the advice of mentors and returned to my original path of becoming a faculty member.

Being a nontraditional full-time graduate student made my studies more interesting. I knew from talking with students who had gone straight through their studies that my work and life experience brought a different, and perhaps fresh, perspective. Inspired by my work with C. Eric Lincoln in my undergraduate years and active in the social-action aspects of black churches, I decided to focus my academic research on church archives. With Lawrence Levine's *Black Culture and Black Consciousness* as a theoretical guide,[13] I would study the impact of churches and congregants on society by analyzing records and exploring whether the specific custodian of these records had an effect on their meaning, interpretation, or value. I spent years justifying my intended dissertation topic and graciously accepting queries about the quality of the education I received from the historically black college I attended. I began teaching at different universities to gain experience and to keep my mind off my discomfort. I have always been one to speak my mind and am often able to find an agreeable solution to what seems unfair or inappropriate, but feeling hazed by faculty at age thirty to obtain this latest degree lacked luster, to say the least. My committee members changed three or four times, but the final straw was the day a faculty member told me that they were scared to be in the same room with me.

Shocked that my experience seemed so much like that of my older mentors, it was clear to me that the academy had not changed enough. Much like the workplace, it was another institution pressured to diversify but unable to truly enact inclusion and genuinely see the benefits of cultural discourse. This systemic rejection is best described as diversity resistance: "a range of practices and behaviors within and by organizations that interfere, intentionally or unintentionally, with the use of diversity as opportunity for learning and effectiveness."[14] Upon the completion of my comprehensive exams, I immediately moved away to a more supportive environment to conduct my research and write my dissertation. Although this move meant that it took me longer to finish, I fondly remember the standing ovation I received when my degree was conferred. It is amazing how early experiences can shape your perspective so easily if you let them. These experiences were some of my first insights into the "other side" of academia, and I walked away with the feeling that academia was full of fake liberals whose curiosities are as insulting as the intentional and unintentional microaggressions that one experiences. I learned that the notion of academia as the place of "true intellectual discourse" is true only to the extent that implicit and explicit biases remain top-of-mind and in check. When allowed to go unchecked, majority institutions can traumatize people of color by the stress and dishonesty and tokenism. It is imperative that people of color create support systems and help each other to endure and finish.[15] We must get the degree, be visible in the ivory tower, and participate.

"GO NORTH—YOU'RE A NEW YORKER, NOT A SOUTHERNER"

While writing my dissertation, I worked as a librarian at a technical college in Georgia. For all of the challenges that working with a skeletal staff each day presented, being able to have such a profound impact on such a diverse student body was inspiring. Technical college seemed like people's first or last chance to change their lives. Every day felt like an opportunity to help someone succeed; in between signing papers for parole officers or social workers, I wanted to ensure each student had what he or she needed to complete a certificate or an associate's degree. I was a newly minted librarian, and this first job allowed me to perform all aspects of librarianship, which undoubtedly made me a stronger candidate for jobs I would compete for later in my career.

Mastering Habit 3, "Put first things first"[16]—when I arrived, there were no written procedures for library operations, little understanding of the role of a librarian, and perhaps even less motivation to understand the role of librarian or library, among the school's executive leadership and instructors. The obvious challenges inspired me to perform and perfect all aspects of librarianship including cataloging, acquisitions, collection development, reference, and instruction. It was through this job that I learned the inner workings of an online catalog, vendor relationships, and the importance of having a collection development plan and faculty input.

By the end of my tenure, the number of staff in the library doubled, and I solidified plans for the library's physical expansion. As much as I enjoyed this job, I knew my ultimate goal was to be an archivist, so I accepted a curatorial position in special collections at a nearby university, handling books and other printed materials.

For all of the comforts of returning to a familiar place, it was often frustrating to feel isolated yet again. It didn't seem like the people around me saw the potential of our department with the same passion that I did. My expertise was questioned. My passion was interpreted as wanting to be in charge; my quietness interpreted as being unfriendly. The work climate was becoming tenser, when all I wanted to do was learn about the profession, hone my skills, and try new things. Perhaps I was overqualified by this point, but my intent was to meaningfully contribute to the organization in more than a rudimentary or mediocre way. I wanted to move the needle by processing collections, addressing backlogs, and expanding our user base. I worked with prestigious donors and negotiated a book donation from a celebrity. I participated in receiving a national leader's papers and collection of books, I processed a local politician's papers that had been on the shelf for decades, and I learned and applied new technologies. Even then, I never quite felt settled.

I started teaching online and began applying for jobs in traditional institutions as well. I failed to land another practitioner position. After being told that my having a doctorate was confusing or uncomfortable for search committee members, I began applying for faculty positions. It was something that a mentor of mine said that changed my course: "Go North—You're a New Yorker, not a Southerner." And with her recommendation I moved to Washington, DC—certainly more north, but definitely still "the South"—and accepted a director position in special collections at a university.

With skills in new technologies, management, customer service, and community relations under my belt, combined with experience with online teaching, library cataloging, digitization, and my archival expertise, I comfortably stepped into this new leadership role. My fresh ideas, new systems, and new attitude were welcomed and met with support.

It was in this position where I began to truly execute Habit 4, "Think win-win",[17] recognizing the value of relationships and the value of building a diverse team for the benefit of not only the individual, but also the collective.

Empowering staff and accepting their differences has always helped me achieve goals beyond my wildest dreams. In order to pursue and complete projects assigned—the ones that fell in my lap and the ones I wanted to pursue because they were interesting to me or the staff—I asked my team to lead. When I arrived we were a staff of five, but by the time I left the department had grown to fourteen, including two endowed positions. By nurturing existing relationships and forming new ones, I was able to participate in the solicitation of a large donation to fund a renovation, which led to my work in university advancement. I raised approximately $4 million, coauthored grants, worked with development officers, and had close conversations with the university president. The exposure I gained from this job was life-changing.

Getting jobs is as much about networking as it is about your qualifications. Sometimes opportunities to grow are masked as failures. Without a few people guiding and encouraging me, I don't know that my professional or personal future would have turned out the same.

Personal and Professional Worlds Collide

Just as my career fell into place, the stability it offered me was shaken by my personal life. I continued to struggle with Habit 7, "Life balance,"[18] and my current hardship illuminated the weight of the geographic distance between my support system and myself. Attempting to achieve the life balance that often seemed to elude me, I accepted a promotion closer to family. The uniqueness of this position was just what I was looking for. It was an opportunity to expand my portfolio and offered an acceptance of a progressive view of the future of libraries. It was an opportunity to manage the life cycle of historic material regardless of the format. This new role would also allow me to steward the existing collection and transition to assisting in the appraisal of born-digital content by assisting researchers with the use of technology and applying digital tools in conducting research.

The team was fragmented and had already endured several reorganizations and shifting of staff roles, but I viewed it as an opportunity for everyone to learn something new. Morale was low, but I was convinced that everyone had something to contribute. I established a digitization program with a lab, was awarded a substantial federal grant—the first of that size in the library—I acquired collections from notable local figures and politicians, and I successfully rekindled relationships with alumni. Just as staff members were beginning to accept new tasks and regain confidence and excitement, organizational politics rose to the surface and decisions were made without consulting me. Amidst my successes and within a few hours, my staff and I endured a surprising restructure of our department, completely unbeknownst to me.

The betrayal inflicted more trauma then I ever could have imagined. Coworkers whom I considered friends kept the secret and in cowardliness and selfishness accepted supervision of one-third of my staff without as much as a courtesy conversation with me. Being the only minority and person excluded from dialogue about my department was a powerful reminder that the "existence of a racial hierarchy that places whites at the top" is still real.[19] I quickly considered the "racialization" or "whitewashing" of the work place, "while cloaking the work place in a culture of informality and business politics."[20]

When the opportunity presented itself to join one of the most diverse leadership teams in an academic library I immediately took it. I knew that the professional scars earned along the way were taking a toll on my personal well-being, but I was not defeated. Under new management, I experienced a shift from internal workplace troubles to external challenges. Our nation was experiencing an explosion of social movements orchestrated by the use of social media. Whatever pessimism or discomfort I was healing from disappeared as my new team and I focused our energies on building a community archive to reflect the feelings and activities of social media users who were participating in these new social movements. Applying my digital and archival skills to preserve this new form of activism was rejuvenating. In the midst of seeking ways to preserve and provide future access to born-digital content that reflected protest activities of the local community, I also became disheartened by the disingenuous people that I continued to encounter in the academy. Yearning for the university community to work within local communities, rather than use them as test or research subjects, it became difficult for me to focus on the collections, the evidence that informs the writing of history. Even under these circumstances, my staff excelled. We were awarded grants, we were doing innovative work, and the team was on a brighter path.

Being an associate university librarian is being middle management and is not quite the same as being at the table directly hearing from the top leaders of the institution. For these reasons, it was not difficult leaving the university setting. Upon request, I interviewed and accepted a position to work for the National Archives Records Administration to preserve and provide access to the records of President and Mrs. Jimmy Carter. My current position has so far proven to be an exciting mix of challenges, rewards, and high expectations, but most rewarding of all has been the autonomy afforded to me due to my diverse skills and background that seemed nontraditional to so many along the way. I am living proof that the road less traveled can still lead to great success.

PAY IT FORWARD

Every day I seek balance—because I am aware that I do not fit in anyone's box. From being the tallest in the class during my childhood to now being one of the oldest moms in my child's classroom, I see the bewilderment and curiosity on people's faces every day. Some choose to boldly ask questions and others just gossip; either way I am fairly certain that people's assumptions of me, personally and professionally, are incomplete. I am motivated to lead by all those who said I couldn't or shouldn't even try. I continue to strive for excellence in leadership to show my supporters, and those who will follow, that it is possible. I did it and so can you. Each rung up the ladder gets lonelier and lonelier, but I am committed to library leadership, specifically, in order to bring diversity, business perspective, contagious energy, effective systems, and qualified people into the profession and into leadership. I am walking advocacy, and I know I make a difference. My journey has been fascinating and has yielded much more personal development and discovery than it has yielded tangible rewards.

The business principles that apply in my daily work have been beneficial and something I hope universities learn to incorporate more than many currently attempt to. I also know that while there has been progress, we are far from the day when I will walk into a boardroom and see a group of leaders that truly reflects the world we live in and the people we serve. At least the shock and longing for someone who looks like me in the room (who isn't filling my water glass) has worn off.

The job is not easier nowadays. I have just gotten older and my circumstances have changed, along with my priorities and interests. It is less about what people think of me, less about whether I can prove myself, less about the stereotypes placed on me, and more about finding peace so I can be joyful at home and at work and ensure that the world continues to see African American women leading powerful organizations and making meaningful decisions. It is important for me to be visible, not only so those who look like me can see their dreams reflected in my journey, but also so those who don't look like me can begin to see black women leaders as a norm, not an exception. I endure so that I may encourage others, open the door for others, and change the minds and influence the behavior of others.

NOTES

1. Peter F. Drucker, *Essential Drucker* (New York: Harper Collins, 2001), p. 204.
2. Kim-Yin Chan and Fritz Drasgow, "Toward a Theory of Individual Differences and Leadership: Understanding the Motivation to Lead," *Journal of Applied Psychology* 86, no. 3 (2001), 481–98, doi:10.1037/0021–9010.86.3.481; Stephen R. Covey, *The 7 Habits of Highly Effective People* (New York: Simon & Shuster, 1990).
3. Chan, Kim-Yin, Yimeng Li, Ho Moon-Ho Ringo, Olexander Chernyshenko, and Yoke Loo Sam, "Three Factors of the Motivation to Lead Affective, Non-calculative and Social Motivation to Lead: What We Know from Studies of Entrepreneurial, Professional and Leadership Motivation" (paper presented at the 16th Congress of the European Association of Work and Organizational Psychology [EAWOP], May 22–25, 2013, Münster, Germany), p. 12 doi:10.13140/2.1.1799 .5529, available from https://www.researchgate.net/profile/Kim_Yin_Chan.
4. Covey, *7 Habits*, p. 65.
5. Ken Blanchard, Patricia Zigarmi, and Drea Zigarmi, *Situational Leadership and the One Minute Manager* (New York: William Morrow, 1999).
6. Paul Hersey, *The Situational Leader*, 4th ed. (Cary, NC: Center for Leadership Studies, 1992).
7. Paul Hersey, "What We Do: Situational Leadership," The Center for Leadership Studies: The Global Home of Situational Leadership, accessed February 2016, https://situational.com/the-cls-difference/situational-leadership-what-we-do/.
8. Blanchard, Zigarmi, and Zigarmi, *Leadership and the One Minute Manager*.
9. Randolph W. Cameron, *The Minority Executives' Handbook* (New York: Harper Collins, 1996).
10. Covey, *7 Habits*, p. 95.
11. Ibid., p. 259–261.
12. Lynne Perry Wooten, Erika Hayes James. "When Firms Fail to Learn The Perpetuation of Discrimination in the Workplace." *Journal of Management Inquiry*, 2004: 23–33 Vol. 13 No. 1, March 2004 (p.23) doi: 10.1177/1056492603259059.
13. Lawrence W. Levine, Black Culture and Black Consciousness: Afro-American Folk Thought from Slavery to Freedom (New York: Oxford University Press, 1978).
14. Kecia M. Thomas and Victoria C. Plaut, "The Many Faces of Diversity Resistance in the Workplace," in *Diversity Resistance in Organizations*, ed. Kecia M. Thomas (New York: Lawrence Erlbaum Associates, 2008), p. 5.
15. Marco J. Barker. "Racial Context, Currency and Connections: Black Doctoral Student and White Faculty Advisor Perspectives on Cross-Race Advising," *Innovations in Education and Teaching International* 48, no. 4 (2011), 387–400, doi:10 .1080/14703297.2011.617092.
16. Covey, *7 Habits*, p. 146.

17. Ibid., p. 205.
18. Ibid., p.289.
19. Stacey J. Lee. "Learning about Race, Learning about 'America,'" in *Beyond Silenced Voices: Class, Race, and Gender in United States Schools*, ed. Michelle Fine and Lois Weis (New York: SUNY Press, 2005), p. 133.
20. Meredith Reitman, "Uncovering the White Place: Whitewashing at Work," *Social and Cultural Geography* 7, no. 2 (2006): p. 267, doi:10.1080/14649360600600692.

BIBLIOGRAPHY

Barker, Marco J. "Racial Context, Currency and Connections: Black Doctoral Student and White Faculty Advisor Perspectives on Cross-Race Advising." *Innovations in Education and Teaching International* 48, no. 4 (2011): 387–400. doi: 10.1080/14703297.2011.617092.

Blanchard, Ken, Patricia Zigarmi, and Drea Zigarmi. *Leadership and the One Minute Manager: Increasing Effectiveness through Situational Leadership*. New York: William Morrow, 1999.

Cameron, Randolph W. *The Minority Executives' Handbook*. New York: Harper Collins, 1996.

Chan, Kim-Yin, and Fritz Drasgow. "Toward a Theory of Individual Differences and Leadership: Understanding the Motivation to Lead." *Journal of Applied Psychology* 86, no. 3 (2001): 481–98. doi:10.1037/0021–9010.86.3.481.

Chan, Kim-Yin, Yimeng Li, Ho Moon-Ho Ringo, Olexander Chernyshenko, and Yoke Loo Sam. "Three Factors of the Motivation to Lead Affective, Non-calculative and Social Motivation to Lead: What We Know from Studies of Entrepreneurial, Professional and Leadership Motivation." Paper presented at the 16th Congress of the European Association of Work and Organizational Psychology (EAWOP), May 22–25, 2013, Münster, Germany. doi:10.13140/2.1.1799.5529. Available from https://www.researchgate.net/profile/Kim_Yin_Chan.

Covey, Stephen R. *The 7 Habits of Highly Effective People*. New York: Simon & Schuster, 1990.

Drucker, Peter F. *Essential Drucker: Management, the Individual and Society*. New York: Harper Collins, 2001.

Hersey, Paul. *The Situational Leader*, 4th ed. Cary, NC: Center for Leadership Studies, 1992.

———. "What We Do: Situational Leadership." The Center for Leadership Studies: The Global Home of Situational Leadership. Accessed February 2016. https://situational.com/the-cls-difference/situational-leadership-what-we-do/.

Lee, Stacey J. "Learning about Race, Learning about 'America.'" In *Beyond Silenced Voices: Class, Race, and Gender in United States Schools*. Edited by Michelle Fine and Lois Weis, 133–45. New York: SUNY Press, 2005.

Levine, Lawrence W. Black Culture and Black Consciousness: Afro-American Folk Thought from Slavery to Freedom. New York: Oxford University Press. 1978.

Reitman, Meredith. "Uncovering the White Place: Whitewashing at Work." *Social and Cultural Geography* 7, no. 2 (2006): 267–82. doi:10.1080/14649360600600692.

Thomas, Kecia M., and Victoria C. Plaut. "The Many Faces of Diversity Resistance in the Workplace." In *Diversity Resistance in Organizations*. Edited by Kecia M. Thomas, 1–22. New York: Lawrence Erlbaum Associates, 2008.

Chapter 7

USING LEADERSHIP TO ACCOMPLISH LONG-TERM GOALS

Hector Escobar

LEADERSHIP AND INSPIRATION come from many sources. What gives one that spark or desire to try something new? Is it because some other library or industry has tried it with successful results? Is it because you see the potential for innovation and positive impact? Whatever that catalyst for leadership and change may be, it needs to be used in a mindful way to accomplish long-term goals. The trajectory toward accomplishing these goals leads to the cultivation of leadership skills over the long term. It is not something that develops overnight, but takes hard work, time, and investment in advancement.

In the past, I used to think of long-distance trips in terms of the final destination, not the journey taken to get there. Perhaps it was my lack of patience with driving or flying, but my focus was always on the destination. I can recall thinking about what I was going to do once I arrived and how best to utilize my time. I would consider scenarios based on changing variables, such as weather. What if it rained when I was planning a hike outside? What if traffic congestion took me off course or delayed my reaching the final destination? Sometimes, it is the unexpected events that make the final destination that much more beautiful and appreciated.

Then I thought librarianship, our collegial network, and the individuals we serve are a lot like that journey to a specific destination. We have so many factors that impact our day-to-day work, but in the end our goal is to accomplish something meaningful and substantial. Just as on a trip, we can take those unexpected events and use them to lead us to our biggest sources of inspiration or most fruitful leadership opportunities. More often, however, that initial glimmer or spark and the foresight to anticipate a need are not always evident. There are many times in our profession when we question along the old adage, if it is not broken, why fix it? Why should we change something if it is functioning? This line of thinking can lead to complacency or stagnation. With this mind set, there is very little forward momentum to improve and certainly not a lot of opportunity for innovation.

How does leadership fit into this? Forward thinking comes by way of many avenues. It comes from networking with colleagues to collaborate and share ideas. It comes from the drive for improvement and that feeling of knowing there is always more to be done. It also comes from our background or cultural experiences and our membership in a minority group. The development and practice of leadership traits for individuals coming from a minority group may be challenging. There are times when being a librarian from an underrepresented group many feel like the cards are stacked against you. Instead of feeling discouraged, leaders need to use this as an opportunity to empower themselves and members of the minority group. What is learned from that experience and how the learning is applied are the most predictive of leadership success.

For me personally, the desire to take on a leadership role was founded on three reasons. Reason one: you have to keep life interesting for yourself and your colleagues. Change may be difficult, but the reality is that it is necessary for the improvement of the organization and profession. Reason two: to dispel the notion of a minority hire. For minority librarians outside of their social enclave, there is sometimes a mind set that they may have been diversity hires. This may come in the form of industry racism if the individuals are typically not from a regional area.[1] A perfect example is the librarian resident, where the librarian hired may know and feel that their employment was due in large part to race or meeting a diversity quota. As ethnic diversification continues to reach across the country, this can be an opportunity to change what leadership looks like and who can serve in that capacity.

Lastly, reason three: there is little or no room for failure. For some minority librarians who may have relocated for employment and who may not have family in the region, the choice is simple. You either make it work, or you move on to something else. However, the tight world of academic librarianship is not always forgiving. The leaders and nonleaders are identified at times having a lasting impact on those in their minority group. Social networks and the perception of minorities both internally and externally can generate forward momentum by capitalizing on positive outcomes nationally, but public failures or shortcomings can influence majority perception of a minority group.[2]

Whatever the reason for seeking out a leadership position, the path one must take is never an easy one and is often fraught with trials. However, led by the drive to improve, advance the perception of minority groups, and build leadership skills, there are some specific steps that can lead to success in accomplishing long-term goals.

SMALL STEPS ADD MILEAGE OVER TIME

When minority librarians are new to the job, regardless of position, we all go through a phase of settling in. This phase usually takes shape by learning how everyone fits into the organization and what role they play. This may be as easy as learning everyone's name, or it may be more in-depth, depending on the complexity of the organization and overlapping functions that may exist in team-based environments.

The length of time in the settling-in phase may differ depending on the organization's structure. However, it is important for every leader to learn the names and functions of most or all employees they encounter within the organization, even those who may not be directly within their department. This not only helps leaders know who to contact and how to get information for various operations quickly, but it also begins the process of establishing your role within the organization and helps build political goodwill. It is important that you, as a minority leader, build a foundation of trust and relationships. A colleague is more likely to remember and respond favorably to someone who knows their name and professional interests and has taken the time to read their bio. Having a few talking points of interest can go a long way in building confidence and laying the foundation for a solid leadership relationship. This is especially important for minority librarians who may need to overcome preconceived beliefs before being perceived as a competent and respected leader. Trying to make changes too quickly without the support, respect, and knowledge of one's collegial network can be more damaging than beneficial. It is important to take as long as needed to lay this necessary foundation.

Following this introductory phase, the leader in each of us needs to ask, how can we contribute to change that has a lasting impact and propels the organization forward? For some, the answer may lie within their own self-interests. After settling in, maintaining the status quo may be acceptable and desirable for some. For others, it may be the desire for change. The aspiration to improve and seek out change is usually the starting point for leadership skills to manifest. For many of us, this is not an easy process. At the end of the day leadership requires us to look at the big picture even when most days it is difficult just simply trying to get through your e-mail inbox.

Management skills take time to build. They involve looking at the big picture, seeing who current and future stakeholders may be, and knowing who has the needed skills for various tasks.[3] This of course goes with approachability, with essentially everyone you work with, regardless of their department. This is why it is important to take time to settle in and learn the politics, strengths, and areas of refinement for each of those individuals in your organization. Knowing this can move projects along faster and remove barriers that may appear if a person is not matched adequately to the tasks they are asked to complete.

In my case, I arrived at an institution where there were pressing space issues, antiquated work processes, and department personnel issues. I was tasked with managing and improving all of these areas while personally trying to meet the needed tenure requirements. After initially settling in and surveying the work ahead, I took a deep breath and said, "Let's do this!" I knew it was going to be an uphill battle, but any leader will know that leading change is never easy. Leadership may get easier over time once the momentum is started and skills are refined, but minority librarians must always keep in mind that we have another barricade to overcome and change will not occur without hard work and changes to perceptions of minorities.

As we began moving down the path to change, there was the realization that despite our differences, we all had shared interest in making the work environment more positive. Think about it this way: no one likes to be stuck out in the cold rain getting soaked. Almost everyone can agree that an umbrella would be an improvement in that particular situation. It is a little more difficult when trying to create a positive work environment because that often means a variety of things to different people. A leader must step back and think, where is the common ground? Where is that umbrella?

In my particular situation, this meant a much needed renovation. However, doing a major renovation of a floor in a public service area is not an overnight process. Depending on funding, this could take several years to plan out and to justify the need. Leading a renovation is a bit like succession planning. There are numerous variables to consider while continuing to plant ideas and make improvements in small steps. Those small steps are all leading toward a larger future goal, which sometimes may be years in the making.

Leading change that may not have immediate impact takes skill and the willingness to learn new things and overcome hurdles. Minority leaders are especially prepared to lead these types of long-term changes due to leadership styles that are often more transformational and include the ability to be more connected to and motivational toward their coworkers while continuing to be long-term goal-oriented.[4] Additionally, minority leaders often have the ability to navigate and remove obstacles that prevent a job from being completed. This is a necessity for projects that may not come to fruition for many years and may be riddled with blockades designed to deter the project from being completed. Minority leaders are often familiar with adversity making them well equipped to endure and ultimately reach long-term goals. This leadership style is different from that of the majority group, which is often very task-oriented and rigid rather than motivational and relationship-oriented. As a result, when the path becomes obscured or tasks are not completed, it is easy for the group to lose sight of the overarching purpose and move in a totally different direction. Minority leaders continue to move toward the end goal and in a common direction despite veering off the path from time to time.

When a leader envisions change that will take place over several years, their worst enemy may be complacency. Complacency may develop with certain accomplishments, such as being awarded tenure or general job satisfaction. If comfort wins out and morphs into unwillingness to change, that could be the downfall for a department or organization and for a long-term goal.[5]

In my particular case, it took nearly seven years to reach our goal of a renovation, with the last year being the fastest and most productive. We were prepared because we took those small steps and were ready to go when the opportunity and funding became available. Along the way we constantly instituted a welcoming and positive environment to match what would eventually be the new space. Data gathering, political goodwill, and planting seeds for possible change all contributed to making the renovation project one of easy acceptance when it was finally launched.

POLITICAL GOODWILL—PLANTING THE SEED

Leadership is good only if the people you work with are on board with you. Sure, it is okay to have a difference of opinion at times, but long-term, good leadership requires people to take interest and follow what you are doing. Librarians of color will be faced with questions when trying to lead individuals or sell an idea, especially if they are from dissimilar backgrounds. In my early career stages of supervising, I often thought I alone had the solutions to fix various problems or concerns that would arise. Ideas or solutions I thought would work sometimes were not popular or would fail. The main reason for this was because I neglected to get input and feedback from the individuals the intended solution would affect. My simple advice...if you do it alone, you are setting yourself up for failure.

Invest the time to talk with others about various projects, even those that may be outside of your own department. They may have ideas or suggestions that people within the department did not consider because they are too close to the situation. Hearing others' thoughts and opinions is a good way to gauge how the proposed ideas would fit in with current practices and may shed light on areas that were not previously considered. Reaching out to others builds social capital.[6] Think of it from the receiving end: someone took the time to take in your suggestions and opinions because they value your input and truly want to make positive changes for everyone. The hope is that in the end this not only fosters a more positive perception, but also encourages a welcoming and more productive social and working environment. Promoting a project or a long-term goal as a leader in a library is comparable to an entrepreneur who must "sell" their ideas to others to establish funding and build support for a product, service, or idea. Oftentimes, a way of doing this is to reach out to others and collect feedback, input, and support. Consider Andrew Mason, the founder for Groupon. He was given one million dollars from his previous employer to develop a unique Web service. Initially, he developed a website called The Point, which focused on social initiatives. After feedback from users that it was too conceptual, he eventually morphed that idea into what we now know as Groupon. In two short years, Mason not only made money back for his investors, but the company did so well it declined a $6 billion acquisition offer from Google in 2010.[7] All of this was possible because of his ability to sell his idea and his reliance on user feedback and input.

In the case of our renovation, the realization of our goal was a collective process. Leadership does not necessarily mean taking the spotlight. It needs to be counterbalanced with modesty and behind-the-scenes motivation to empower the staff to lead in their respective areas. A good leader needs to have the skills to mobilize their team, energize them, and provide direction (even if years out) for fulfilling the future aspirations of the library.[8] A good leader will walk with their staff along the way, but let them finish on their own and garner their own acknowledgment.

Whether it be with a faculty liaison or the spouse of a dean or provost, a good leader will need to network both within and outside of the library. Just like politics, knowing who knows who, and in what capacity, is vital for how the library is viewed by its external stakeholders. For example, if you have a campus administrator who supports an idea you have, you are likely to find the needed resources faster than simply mentioning it to a colleague over lunch. Do not be afraid to engage with others if and when opportunities arise. Use your social skills to inject yourself wherever possible to tell your stories and your ideas to others.

For a minority leader, fostering these relationships through networking opportunities is especially vital to advancing perceptions of the minority group as well as developing support and social capital. Having strong social capital, not just within one's department, but throughout the campus or organization, makes change efforts more efficient and easier to initiate since the foundation has already been constructed. People are resources, ultimately your most valuable resources. These resources are established by forming relationships, for which there is a common goal of betterment or purpose. A simple, common example of this would be a neighborhood watch program. Typically one or a few neighbors will take interest in wanting to secure a neighborhood. In order for the program to work, though, it requires leaders of the program to have everyone on board and for each neighbor to be vigilant of their surroundings.

Within an academic library setting, social capital may exist with the establishment of relationships between external departments. At my current library, for example, we formed a relationship with the honors program on campus. Students from this program are allowed access to private study spaces in the library. In turn, the program funds three intern positions for the library to use for work on various projects.

DATA HAS NO COLOR LINES, BUT IT DOES SHINE BRIGHTLY

Leadership not only includes aspects of social capital, political goodwill, and the human side to accomplishing goals, but it also relies on hard evidence that supports an argument or direction. We find this in the form of data. Reliance on data is imperative when time or resources are limited. Politicians, for example, are always touting statistics and figures to illustrate a point. They realize they have limited time to persuade an audience; they do so by showcasing quick, yet powerful figures.

Data or numbers generated by businesses or organizations are simply just that, numbers. A people counter at the front door does not tally how many minorities or males and females have entered a building. It tells us only how many individuals have entered. Data can paint a picture, but it must be used in the context of previous data gathered to determine its relevance. In the library world we call this assessment, where data is compared or assessed over time to reveal changes, or in some cases opportunities.

Data collected within our profession can sometimes be overwhelming. We collect data on the number of books that are circulated, individuals using public computers, how many questions were answered via phone, e-mail, and more…the list is endless. Instead, data should be analyzed, referenced, and used for decision making. As leaders in our profession, we need to paint the picture of progress and accomplishment. One tool that is used within educational leadership and decision making is the Cycle of Formative Data-Based Decision Making.[9] It consists of five elements: identify, plan, apply, assess, and refine. The model was originally developed for the educational setting to provide a method or structure for making decisions. It is imperative that when making decisions, all stakeholders be on the same page about how those decisions will be made, affording them the opportunity to be active participants in the process. Reliance on data and its use within the context of the Formative Data-Based Decision Making helps to identify needs and refine the focus of leaders. It also separates assessment processes into more manageable steps to evaluate progress towards a goal.

Let's examine the five elements. Data identification looks to showcase patterns, resolving anecdotal claims, and looks for trends. Planning revolves around setting your own goal or purpose and how the data factors into this. Applying is the execution of the actual change element or process. Assessing, of course, is evaluating the impact of the new process or change and examining the new set of data collected. Finally, refining is the end of the cycle but also a look to the future whereby we try to answer what could be changed for even better outcomes or improvement.

So often, libraries adopt new services to keep up with the innovations of other libraries rather than analyzing local data and finding what is best for their institution. Have you ever noticed that many library websites tend to look alike? Or have you heard of new services launched because it was mentioned that another library was doing something similar? The cautionary note for leaders is to not just dive into something because it is trendy or another colleague suggested it would be popular. Rather, determine the needs of your local institution by examining data and using a process like the Cycle of Formative Data-Based Decision Making to establish something that is unique to your own institution.

Using the case study of our renovation that was discussed previously, data was gathered over time and spoke strongly of our students' need for more space within the library. We then took this need and looked at opportunities within our library to combine functional spaces, thus freeing the necessary area elsewhere.

What data was collected and used for us to justify our renovation? To name a few, we used hourly floor counts of various floors, usage data for resources used within our reference collection (used for deaccessioning), types and frequency of questions that came in through our service areas, LibQUAL+ results, and comments from two iterations of campus-wide surveys. Additionally, since we were considering relocating a service in the library that was staffed by an external department, we asked if we could analyze data collected by that department to see where the library could fit in and if operations could be consolidated or combined in order to open more spaces for students.

The important thing to note is that librarians of color who wish to become future leaders need to understand the importance of data and use it effectively. Identifying the need for a new library service or seeking funding for new positions needs to be supported by data. Having data can often be the impetus to strengthen claims and requests to upper management. Although using data to inform change and evaluate processes in the library is a necessity, as leaders we still need to use other tactics to as an impetus to lead and help tell our stories more effectively. We do this by sharing regular updates, giving progress reports, and presenting to both internal and external stakeholders.

Lessons Learned

As librarians of color, we as leaders must acknowledge that at times we will have an uphill battle with lots of bumps in the road. Minorities who are not a part of the normal functional operation are often questioned, perceived as incapable, and sometimes disregarded based on race and their standing within the institution or organization.[10]

Failure is one stumbling block that all true leaders must come to accept, and at times welcome. Not everything will turn out great...projects may and will fail, people and staff transition to other departments or institutions, ideas come and go, and sometimes supporters of your project may abruptly jump ship. It is how we learn from our failures and adapt that allows us to try again and avoid mistakes in the future.

Be flexible. There will be days when what you hoped to accomplish on a project will not happen. There will be days where you lose your battle to prove your point at a meeting. Rather than give in and move on to something else, think about what you might want to do differently to effect change. For example, if you normally host meetings at your office or in your department, try asking others to call the meeting, allow them to set the agenda, and meet them on their turf. You will notice that if other parties feel valued, they may feel more inclined to accept your ideas. A real leader does not need to meet on their grounds in order to be effective.

Above all, do not meet for the sake of meeting. Excessive meetings can increase stress and cause loss of team productivity.[11] Limit agenda items to what is feasible. Think about what you can communicate via e-mail, rather than what is needed in person. Try a divide-and-conquer approach. Rather than meeting as a whole group, try meeting individually to get your point across and build rapport. See where there may be variance between individuals and tweak your selling points so that you may adapt to specific interests. That way, when you do meet as a group, each person feels invested in the project.

Communicate and seek mentors. As librarians we are blessed to be in a field of ever-evolving professional development and networking opportunities. Whether those are regional venues like state library association workshops, or larger venues such as ACRL or ALA national conferences, we use the time to learn from others and catch up with colleagues from other institutions. Share your experiences and ask questions of individuals who you feel are trustworthy. Use these opportunities to get and share ideas, collaborate, even work on projects. In fact, collaboration, even on written projects, seems to strengthen articles written by more than one author from more than one institution.[12]

Perhaps the most important part of communication is the art of listening. In our profession we sometimes get carried away with telling our stories and accomplishments to others. Think about it. It's very common to hear at conferences, "Oh…our library does this cool thing" or, "I just wrote this article on…" Instead, take a step back and take the time to listen. Most importantly, listen to your staff and colleagues. When you listen, you are taking a breath and the time to formulate new ideas and directions. How you listen and respond will vary with each person you encounter. You may not be overly excited about the small talk and wanting to hear about what someone did over the weekend. But if you are actively listening, you are showing that you care about that person and are willing to take the time to know and learn about what interests them. Again, it ties back to social capital. Being a good leader requires you to listen and talk to all walks of life and to make individuals feel like they matter. Watching a director speaking with their management staff down one hall, then turning the corner to greet a member of housekeeping by name and engage them in conversation about weekend plans or family is the hallmark of a great leader building social relationships and capital.

One thing that I have learned through the years is to empower the heart. For me, this was a weakness in my leadership development, but one I knew was important to develop. Since people and staff are resources, it is important to value them. Tell them thank you for their accomplishments and contributions, even for the small stuff. If you make people feel valued, even if they are part of a collective and their contributions may be small, they will be more receptive to your ideas and directions in the future since they know that what they do matters to you.

Never get too comfortable. Our profession is one that involves constant change. Technology and changing demographics contribute to the needs and demands of our resources. For some librarians, achieving tenure or promotion may lead to complacency. And while complacency may not be a bad thing in of itself, becoming too comfortable in a certain environment creates resistance to change and prevents adapting to changing demands in the future.[13] In my current environment, change is constant, and it is actually normal to expect changes to staffing, services, and resources every academic year or, in some cases, even semester to semester.

As minority librarians, we have a commitment to advance our colleagues of color. However, in order to be effective within our profession, we must dive into other areas that are beyond our normal enclaves. It is all right to build great working relationships with colleagues who are from the majority or from other backgrounds. It is also acceptable to work on teams and projects that reach beyond the realm of diversity. Showcasing to the library community expertise on aspects that extend beyond diversity must remain your goal. Above all, do not rely on diversity to make a name for future ambitions; let your accomplishments do that for you.[14]

CONCLUSION

Acquiring and strengthening leadership skills and putting them into practice is by no means an overnight process. It requires us to examine our environments and to seek out opportunities. It requires us to dive in, network, build relationships, and lead. As minority librarians, we must often work harder to dispel preconceptions, but the reward is advancement of our libraries, our profession, and our minority groups. Proving ourselves based on accomplishments rather than the color of our skin requires and gives us the unique opportunity to take on projects and lead change on a greater level than just within the library. It is how we develop and advance our leadership skills, learn from our failures, and motivate others to long-term success that will be our legacy as minority leaders. Get out of your comfort zone, lead, and showcase to the rest of the library community and beyond what you can do, especially as a minority librarian.

NOTES

1. Camila A. Alire, "Diversity and Leadership: The Color of Leadership," *Journal of Library Administration* 32, no. 3–4 (2001): 99–114.
2. Ann K. Brooks and Tamara Clunis, "Where to Now? Race and Ethnicity in Workplace Learning and Development Research: 1980–2005," *Human Resource Development Quarterly* 18, no. 2 (Summer 2007): 229–51.
3. Maggie Farrell, "Lifecycle of Library Leadership," *Journal of Library Administration* 53, no. 4 (2013): 255–64.
4. Alexandre Ardichvili, James A. Mitchell, and Douglas Jondle, "Characteristics of Ethical Business Cultures," *Journal of Business Ethics* 85, no. 4 (2009): 445–51.
5. Marco Tavanti and Patricia H. Werhane, "On Complacency, Corporate Cliffs and Power Distance: Global Leadership Ethics from Gender and Cultural Studies Perspectives," *Leadership and the Humanities* 1, no. 1 (September 2013): 22–30.
6. Kenneth W. Koput and Joseph P. Broschak, *Social Capital in Business* (Cheltenham, UK; Northampton, MA: Elgar Research Collection, 2010).
7. Christopher Steiner, "Groupon's Andrew Mason Did What Great Founders Do," *Forbes*, February 28, 2013, http://www.forbes.com/sites/christophersteiner/2013/02/28/groupons-andrew-mason-did-what-great-founders-do/#76adb8e64255.
8. Barbara I. Dewey, "Leadership and University Libraries: Building to Scale at the Interface of Cultures," *Journal of Library Administration* 42, no. 1 (2005): 41–50.
9. Karen Sanzo, John Caggiano, and Steve Myran, *Formative Assessment Leadership* (New York: Routledge, 2015).
10. Katherine T. U. Emerson and Mary C. Murphy, "Identity Threat at Work: How Social Identity Threat and Situational Cues Contribute to Racial and Ethnic Disparities in the Workplace," *Cultural Diversity and Ethnic Minority Psychology* 20, no. 4 (October 2014): 508–20.
11. Stephen Xavier, "Slow Death by Meeting," *Employment Relations Today* 35, no. 3 (Fall 2008): 9–15.
12. Richard L. Hart, "Collaboration and Article Quality in the Literature of Academic Librarianship," *Journal of Academic Librarianship* 33, no. 2 (2007): 190–5.

13. John Kotter, "Leading Change," *Leadership Excellence* 30, no. 2 (February 2013): 6.
14. R. Roosevelt Thomas Jr., "Making Diversity Pay Off," *Leader to Leader* 1998, no. 7 (Winter 1998): 14–16.

BIBLIOGRAPHY

Alire, Camila A. "Diversity and Leadership: The Color of Leadership." *Journal of Library Administration* 32, no. 3–4 (2001): 99–114.

Ardichvili, Alexandre, James A. Mitchell, and Douglas Jondle. "Characteristics of Ethical Business Cultures." *Journal of Business Ethics* 85, no. 4 (2009): 445–51.

Brooks, Ann K., and Tamara Clunis. "Where to Now? Race and Ethnicity in Workplace Learning and Development Research: 1980–2005." *Human Resource Development Quarterly* 18, no. 2 (Summer 2007): 229–51.

Dewey, Barbara I. "Leadership and University Libraries: Building to Scale at the Interface of Cultures." *Journal of Library Administration* 42, no. 1 (2005): 41–50.

Emerson, Katherine T. U., and Mary C. Murphy. "Identity Threat at Work: How Social Identity Threat and Situational Cues Contribute to Racial and Ethnic Disparities in the Workplace." *Cultural Diversity and Ethnic Minority Psychology* 20, no. 4 (October 2014): 508–20.

Farrell, Maggie. "Lifecycle of Library Leadership." *Journal of Library Administration* 53, no. 4 (2013): 255–64.

Hart, Richard L. "Collaboration and Article Quality in the Literature of Academic Librarianship." *Journal of Academic Librarianship* 33, no. 2(2007): 190–5.

Koput, Kenneth W., and Joseph P. Broschak. *Social Capital in Business.* Cheltenham, UK; Northampton, MA: Elgar Research Collection, 2010.

Kotter, John. "Leading Change." *Leadership Excellence* 30, no. 2 (February 2013): 6.

Sanzo, Karen, John Caggiano, and Steve Myran. *Formative Assessment Leadership: Identify, Plan, Apply, Assess, Refine.* New York: Routledge, 2015.

Steiner, Christopher. "Groupon's Andrew Mason Did What Great Founders Do." *Forbes,* February 28, 2013. http://www.forbes.com/sites/christophersteiner/2013/02/28/groupons-andrew-mason-did-what-great-founders-do/#76adb8e64255.

Tavanti, Marco, and Patricia H. Werhane. "On Complacency, Corporate Cliffs and Power Distance: Global Leadership Ethics from Gender and Cultural Studies Perspectives." *Leadership and the Humanities* 1, no. 1 (September 2013): 22–30.

Thomas Jr., R. Roosevelt. "Making Diversity Pay Off." *Leader to Leader* 1998, no. 7 (Winter 1998): 14–16.

Xavier, Stephen. "Slow Death by Meeting." *Employment Relations Today* 35, no. 3 (Fall 2008): 9–15.

Chapter 8[*]

COMMUNITY BUILDING FOR SUCCESS

Jody Gray

AM I SUCCESSFUL? If so, what has motivated my success? Those are tough questions to answer. I would like to have a simple checklist that could help fellow American Indian or other librarians of color,[1] but I don't. What I can offer are some insights into successful strategies used to develop my own leadership skills.

From the very beginning of my higher education journey, I have been influenced by recruitment and retention strategies—beginning with the college recruitment that shaped where I went to school and ending with the position of Diversity Outreach Librarian, a position only I have held at my institution.

Primarily, building personal relationships with mentors and academic support staff are some of the biggest reasons for my success. These relationships, along with my own self-motivation, continue to influence the work that I do developing partnerships and programming in an academic library.

In this chapter, I will walk through some of the strategies that motivated my success becoming a librarian. I will use current research to show how these early influences have impacted my motivations to succeed in this profession. I hope this will give some insight into the value of lived experiences in developing leadership skills and successfully caring for oneself.

RECRUITMENT AND RETENTION STRATEGIES

American Indians in higher education continue to be a small group. The data shows that American Indians are still one of the lowest represented groups in four-year colleges with an average of less than 1 percent of the student body.[2] It is common, but not mandatory, for four-year colleges and universities to invest in outreach and support for American Indian students as part of the outreach to students of color and the pursuit of developing a diverse campus.

I was a first-generation Lakota college student that grew up on the reservation. By the time I was looking at colleges, I had traveled outside of South Dakota and North Dakota only once for a school trip to Washington DC. My entire life, I witnessed so many people from my reservation leave for college, only to return within a few weeks or months, and many never left at all. Ultimately, I was not a great candidate for successfully completing a four-year degree. I had no experience off of the reservation, I did not know what would be expected of me at college, most of my peers did not complete their degrees, and I did not have any money saved to pay for my education.

My first real encounter with a successful recruitment strategy came from a recruiter from the University of Minnesota, Morris (UMM) campus. He came to my high school my senior year. At the time, I had no idea what I should be looking for in a college experience. The UMM recruiter walked me through the process of applying to their school while answering questions and bringing up issues that I never would have thought to ask about, such as financial support.

It is this individualized support from the recruiter and school guidance counselors that provided the skills I needed to apply and choose a college. Farmer-Hinton discussed how students of color who have access to more hands-on college planning networks (guidance counselors, teachers, recruiters, etc.) are more successful at getting in to college.[3]

My first quarter at college was socially more difficult than I would have imagined. I went from being surrounded by all Natives to being the only one in most groups or classes. I found myself driving six hours one way EVERY weekend to see my family and friends and needing to talk myself into returning each Sunday. I did not have any experience interacting outside my small community.

A common theme found the literature centers around the importance of community and identity in retaining American Indian students. In 2012, the Association for the Study of Higher Education (ASHE) published a report titled *Postsecondary Education for American Indian and Alaska Natives* that highlights decade's worth of literature. This source breaks down known recruitment and retention issues.[4]

Despite getting off to a rocky start, I did receive a bachelor's degree in four years. My success in graduating college was directly influenced by the outreach methods that involved building community with the Minority Resource Center at UMM. The coordinator who reached out to me was Native, and I was relieved to have a space and a person who I could approach about my struggles. It would be years before I really looked back and realized that community building was a big factor in my success at college. Along with the sense of community, I felt there was a place I belonged. Doan explored how student involvement in student organizations may have a positive impact on retaining students of color. In this piece, he discussed how students of color often have to detach from their personal culture when attending predominantly white institutions.[5] I was both given and motivated to pursue leadership opportunities in the student organization that helped me develop a bit more self-confidence and continue building community.

Those initial recruitment and retention efforts in college really affected the way that I find ways to motivate myself. Building community became a priority for me. I believe it is a very basic need that is often forgotten as one enters their professional career. I also developed the ability to motivate myself. These are the two skills I have developed that continue to help me succeed in the library profession. I will demonstrate how this played out in my early career.

CONNECTIONS AND COMMUNITY

After I graduated I found myself in brand-new territory once again, a first-generation college graduate. I had no idea what to do next. I struggled in the "real world" because suddenly all of that support and intention about helping me succeed was no longer there.

There is also the harsh reality that when you are seeking a job to pay the bills, there is no recruitment or retention work based on your identity. The expectation is that you will be competent and willing to learn, but how you motivate yourself to be those things is left to the individual. The status as a first-generation college graduate does not go away with your diploma. It took me a couple of years to figure that what I wanted was a career and not a job. I decided to pursue my master's in library science.

One of the lessons I learned as an undergraduate that still holds true today was that I needed support to succeed. Whether that support came as work opportunities, academic support, financial support, or cultural programming, I needed a community in order to succeed. In graduate school, this played out a bit differently. Most of the support services for American Indians or students of color at my institution were focused on undergraduate experiences.

I reached out to a person who worked at the Smithsonian's National Museum of Natural History (NMNH) who was also from the Cheyenne River Sioux Tribe. I did not know this person or her family, but I thought I would reach out because of our tribal connection. She did not work in the libraries, but she forwarded my inquiry to the librarian at the Anthropology Library for NMNH. I think it would have been easy to dismiss my random e-mail, but I am aware of a strong sense of relationships in the Native community. That was a valuable resource to me, and I know that it influences the decisions I make in my career and where I choose to expend my energy.

The internship at the Smithsonian was important in another way. It was exposure to a community of American Indian professionals. It was the first time in my life that I ever met so many American Indians with advanced degrees working off the reservation, but still contributing to their communities, as their work focused on American Indian conservation and repatriation. It was inspiring. It did not matter that they were not librarians, it mattered that they were professionals with advanced degrees. Even if you are not in an area where there are lots of librarians of color, finding community with other professionals of color can have a positive impact.

It is these cohorts of colleagues that I call to help me problem solve or provide support, as we all work for large, predominantly white institutions. This experience is one that helped me address some of my own identity and self-confidence issues. In many ways, this was my first experience with peer mentoring.

INTENTIONAL MENTORS

When I was in graduate school I had a more formal mentorship relationship with the Multicultural Studies Librarian for whom I interned. Michelle Harrell is an African American librarian, and she provided my first real introduction into the world of professional librarians who do work in diversity.

She was an effective mentor, and she did motivate me to start looking more seriously at work in diversity in academic libraries. Although I was a student, Michelle treated me as an equal. She and I applied for a Minority Research Grant from ALA's Office for Diversity and got it. We worked on the project together, even after I had graduated and moved on to my first professional job in Minnesota.

Michelle introduced me to the American Library Association. In return, I began to gather a new community. This time it was not solely American Indians, but librarians of color. Whether she was aware of it or not, what she was doing was demonstrating "social capital."

There are several definitions and frameworks for discussing social capital. In this case, I am referring to social capital in relation to organization studies. Nahapeit wrote, "Social capital refers to the set of resources that accrue to an actor through the actor's social relationships. It thus describes the value of social connections, showing how some individuals and social collectives do better because they better connect with others."[6] With no direct reports or high-level position on an organization chart, Michelle was demonstrating how to lead by using influence and building your social capital.

In 2002, Michelle took me with her to the Diversity: Building a Strategic Future Conference for Academic Libraries at the University of Iowa. It was at this conference that I first heard about residency programs. As someone whose only experience working in the profession was my academic internships, a residency program sounded perfect for my getting my foot in the door of the profession.

Residency programs have been around for over twenty years. According to the ACRL Residency Interest Group, a residency is a "post-degree work experience designed as an entry level program for recent graduates of an MLS program."[7] Each one is organized to fit its particular institution, but many of them were developed specifically to recruit underrepresented minorities (URM). According to Perez, Campbell, and Collins, American Indians make up the smallest number of residents.[8]

Residencies provide opportunity to build professional skills and experience. After graduating with my MLS, I looked for jobs all over the Midwest, as staying in close proximity to my family in South Dakota was a priority. I did not have many interviews. First of all, I did not have much experience, and second, I had no experience in selling myself as a professional. I could sell myself as someone who needed and wanted to continue learning more and having experiences to improve myself as a professional. In 2003, I became a resident at the University of Minnesota.

The program I participated in was structured to include a mentor from the professional staff. My mentor here used a mentoring strategy that focused on "psychosocial aspects" of the mentoring relationship. Manderneck and Richardson described this as "deliberate attention [given] to providing mechanisms that would help the [resident] identify and take advantage of campus and community resources, support networks, and the like to support their transition to the new community."[9]

She looked beyond professional development and was very intentional about connecting me with lots of people across the libraries, across campus, and across the profession at large. With her guidance I was able to make connections to many people who were influential, due to either power role or just personality. Once again, building on my social capital.

INFORMAL MENTORSHIP

In addition to (or sometimes instead of) formal mentoring programs, informal mentoring is part of community building. It can be beneficial to have mentors who are not in the libraries. Aiko Moore, Miller, Pitchford, and Jeng stated, "External mentors help the mentee to avoid workplace conflicts of interest, can be more objective in their observations of difficult internal relationships and offer unique perspectives on how to handle these conflicts in a mentee's time of need."[10] As you move through your career, try different methods, both formal and informal, to identify what works best for you.

PROFESSIONAL COMMUNITIES

Everything I had learned from my undergraduate and graduate experiences taught me the importance of community building in my success. As a quiet, introverted person, it was never easy to reach out to strangers; however, I also knew that as I continued in my profession, I was the only person who would be motivated to take action in identifying and reaching out to this new community.

I would say that in all of the areas that I have succeeded, so far, there has been a connection to a larger American Indian community. At the University of Minnesota, I found the Circle of Indigenous Nations (COIN), the office that supports American Indian students on campus. I just walked through the doors one day and introduced myself to the professional staff. I found another community.

I would advise American Indian and other librarians of color to find a community. No matter where your career takes you, find your community. It can be your personal community or a professional one. Sometimes, you will have only one or the other. Identify offices that support the community you wish to cultivate and introduce yourself to the staff. Attend events put on by your institution or within the community. In addition to helping sustain your own success, often community building can directly impact the organization you work for in a positive way by creating new partnerships with offices or groups that may not have existed before. It may also provide informal mentors to support your success.

BUILD LEADERSHIP SKILLS

Another recommendation is to build your leadership skills. Leadership skills can be learned; not all leadership looks the same. One must build on basic business/professional leadership skills, while recognizing that most librarians of color also have their unique cultural leadership skills that have been learned throughout their lifetime.

Martha Mcleod writes about American Indian leadership. She re-
counted a conversation with Barbra Wakshul about Indian leadership:

> [Indian leadership] is different in the following ways:
> (a) Indian leaders need to know both their own commu-
> nity (values and history) as well as the Euro American
> community because they must function in both societ-
> ies; (b) Indian leaders need to be holistic because Indian
> communities are small, Indians value interconnected-
> ness, and Indians work on a wide variety of issues; (c)
> Indian leaders belong to communal societies that must
> accommodate broth tribal values and Euro-American
> system in which Indians and non-Indians coexist.[11]

Successful librarians of color have learned to harness both sets of
leadership skills and to continue learning and developing new leadership
skills.

I advise librarians to always continue building their leadership skills.
My first professional experience in building leadership skills was part of
the Minnesota Residency. I participated in the University of Minnesota
Institute for Early Career Librarians from Groups Underrepresented in
the Profession. This week-long institute was developed in 1998 and was
initially funded through a US Department of Education Grant. Peggy
Johnson noted,

> The institute had, from the beginning, a twofold focus:
>
> - Institute participants are given a forum for leadership
>   development and increased understanding of them-
>   selves and behavior in complex organizations, and
>   presented opportunities to explore practical skills in
>   key areas for librarians.
>
> - In addition, participants gain a community of peers
>   with whom they develop a support network that is
>   intended to continue through their professional ca-
>   reers.[12]

By far, this was one of the most rewarding leadership institutes I have attended. I would confirm that the goals for this institute are met. As I have mentioned throughout this chapter, community building is a strong part of my motivation and commitment to work. This institute gave me another community of new professionals that continues to influence my work. As I am involved with the profession nationally, I continue to see my colleagues from my year and all of the years in leadership positions.

SELF-MOTIVATION

Self-motivation is another skill you can cultivate in order to learn to know what you need to succeed and advocate for yourself. The institute, along with my remaining years as a resident, gave me experience as a professional and insight as a leader to advocate for what I wanted. I was assigned many roles during my time as a resident. I worked in cataloging, digital reference, arts, humanities, and social sciences reference and physical science reference. Through all of those assignments I maintained a relationship with the COIN, because it was important to me. This was a relationship I developed on my own, not as part of an assignment.

I offered some services directly from the library to COIN after I discovered they did not have a formal relationship with the libraries. I felt like I could provide some support while finding my community. It was in this action that I began to see the impact that programs like COIN were a big part of my success in graduating from college. I felt like I was giving back to my community by supporting students who were reflections of me as a new college student. That is another motivating factor that I have discovered.

I have much empathy for these students and, because of that, I am passionate about the work that I do on their behalf. That motivates me to articulate the importance of my role and the services I provide to this population. The way that I do that is by really trying to understand my organization. My work provides me the space to discuss systems of oppression that are in place within big American institutions. As I learn more about the motivations (both intentional and unintentional), it gives me insights into how to spend my energy within the organization. Those discussions have also exposed me to some incredible allies, and it is their support that I seek when I am feeling frustrated. I have to be motivated to seek that support out, though. It is not going to come to me. It is scary being vulnerable in that way, but it's part of taking care of me. And taking care of one's self is one of the best ways to succeed in any profession.

Conclusion

As I move forward in my career, there are days that continue to challenge me, as I am aware of frustrations and obstacles that will continue to move into my path. I won't lie and say that there are not days that I want to just quit. That being said, I don't and I probably won't, because I have all of these communities of people that I care about and who are also working hard to do the best they can where they are. I do feel that responsibility to my community to support those who are coming after me. I know that I won't win every battle, but more importantly, I know that I have community and that my actions are meaningful. I encourage you to find yours.

Notes

1. Throughout this chapter I will be using the terms *American Indian, Native,* and *Indians* interchangeably.
2. *Chronicle of Higher Education,* "Racial and Ethnic Representation among College Students, by Type of Institution, 2012," *Almanac of Higher Education 2014* (Washington, DC: Chronicle of Higher Education, 2015), http://chronicle.com/article/RacialEthnic/147373/.
3. Raquel Farmer-Hinton, "Social Capital and College Planning: Students of Color Using School Networks for Support and Guidance," *Education and Urban Society* 41, no. 1 (2008): 127–57.
4. Bryan McKinley Jones Brayboy, Amy J. Fann, Angelina E. Castagno, and Jessica A. Solyom, *Postsecondary Education for American Indian and Alaska Natives,* ASHE Higher Education Report 37:5 (San Francisco: Jossey-Bass, 2012).
5. Jimmy Doan, "The Impact of Campus Climate and Student Involvement on Students of Color," *Vermont Connection* 32 (2011): 31–39.
6. Janine Nahapiet, "Social Capital," in *International Encyclopedia of Organization Studies,* vol. 4, ed. Stewart R. Clegg and James R. Bailey (Thousand Oaks, CA: Sage, 2008), 1424–1427.
7. Residency Interest Group website, Association of College and Research Libraries, accessed March 7, 2015, http://acrl.ala.org/residency/.
8. Megan Zoe Perez, Damon Campbell, and Shantree Collins, "The Residents

Report," in *The New Graduate Experience: Post-MLS Residency Programs and Early Career Librarians*, ed. Megan Zoe Perez and Cindy A. Gruwell (Santa Barbara, CA: Libraries Unlimited, 2011), 115.

9. Scott Mandernack and Rebecca A. Richardson, "Program Management: Challenges and Lessons Learned: Purdue University," in *The New Graduate Experience: Post-MLS Residency Programs and Early Career Librarians*, ed. Megan Zoe Perez and Cindy A. Gruwell (Santa Barbara, CA: Libraries Unlimited, 2011), 61.

10. Alanna Aiko Moore et al., "Mentoring in the Millennium: New Views, Climate and Actions," *New Library World* 109, no. 1 (2008): 77.

11. Martha McLeod, "Keeping the Circle Strong: Learning about Native American Leadership," *Tribal College* 13, no. 4 (Summer 2002): 10.

12. Peggy Johnson, "Retaining and Advancing Librarians of Color," *College and Research Libraries* 68, no. 5 (2007): 405–17.

BIBLIOGRAPHY

Aiko Moore, Alanna, Michael J. Miller, Veronda J. Pitchford, and Ling Hwey Jeng. "Mentoring in the Millennium: New Views, Climate and Actions." *New Library World* 109, no. 1 (2008): 75–86.

Brayboy, Bryan McKinley Jones, Amy J. Fann, Angelina E. Castagno, and Jessica A. Solyom. *Postsecondary Education for American Indian and Alaska Natives: Higher Education for Nation Building and Self-Determination*. ASHE Higher Education Report 37:5. San Francisco: Jossey-Bass, 2012.

Brewer, Julie. "Early Career Development and Post-master's Residency Programs." In *The New Graduate Experience: Post-MLS Residency Programs and Early Career Librarianship*. Edited by Megan Zoe Perez and Cindy A. Gruwell, 1–10. Santa Barbara, CA: Libraries Unlimited, 2011.

Chronicle of Higher Education. "Racial and Ethnic Representation among College Students, by Type of Institution, 2012." *Almanac of Higher Education 2014*. Washington, DC: Chronicle of Higher Education, 2015. http://chronicle.com/article/RacialEthnic/147373/.

Doan, Jimmy. "The Impact of Campus Climate and Student Involvement on Students of Color." *Vermont Connection* 32 (2011): 31–39.

Farmer-Hinton, Raquel. "Social Capital and College Planning: Students of Color Using School Networks for Support and Guidance." *Education and Urban Society* 41, no. 1 (2008): 127–57.

Johnson, Peggy. "Retaining and Advancing Librarians of Color." *College and Research Libraries* 68, no. 5 (2007): 405–17.

Mandernack, Scott, and Rebecca A. Richardson. "Program Management: Challenges and Lessons Learned: Purdue University." In *The New Graduate Experience: Post-MLS Residency Programs and Early Career Librarians*. Edited by Megan Zoe Perez and Cindy A. Gruwell, 61–80. Santa Barbara, CA: Libraries Unlimited, 2011.

McLeod, Martha. "Keeping the Circle Strong: Learning about Native American Leadership." *Tribal College* 13, no. 4 (Summer 2002): 10.

Nahapiet, Janine. "Social Capital." In *International Encyclopedia of Organization Studies*, vol. 4. Edited by Stewart R. Clegg and James R. Bailey, 1423–26. Thousand Oaks, CA: Sage Publications, 2008.

Perez, Megan Zoe, Damon Campbell, and Shantree Collins. "The Residents Report." In *The New Graduate Experience: Post-MLS Residency Programs and Early Career Librarians*. Edited by Megan Zoe Perez and Cindy A. Gruwell, 115–36. Santa Barbara, CA: Libraries Unlimited, 2011.

Residency Interest Group website. Association of College and Research Libraries. Accessed March 7, 2015. http://acrl.ala.org/residency/.

Chapter 9

PUBLIC SERVICE
A Foundation of Leadership
Development and Attainment

Binh P. Le

IN MAY 2015, I received an email from the chair of the Nominating Committee of the American Library Association informing me that I have been recommended as a potential candidate for the presidency of the American Library Association. A few weeks earlier, I was notified that I was chosen to be one of the three 2015–16 Pennsylvania State University Administrative Fellows as well as a 2015–16 Center on Institutional Cooperation Academic Leadership Program Fellow.[1] Both of these highly competitive and prestigious fellowships are designed to cultivate future leaders in higher education. Since their inception a few decades ago, many of these programs have produced fellows who have become university presidents, chancellors, and deans. While many factors have contributed to my leadership achievements, including formal education, determination, hard work, perseverance, luck, family and institutional support, research and scholarship, and so on, I do believe that one of the most critical aspects has been my public service record. More specifically, it has been my public contributions to the libraries and the universities where I have worked, the library profession as a whole, and the organizations and institutions outside higher education.

BACKGROUND

I first learned about the importance of public service before I graduated from library school. It happened during my library practicum (internship) at Purdue University in West Lafayette, Indiana. It was here where the head of the department told me, among many other insightful aspects of librarianship, about the importance of public service as it related to my future career development. In particular, he encouraged me to actively engage in the activities of the American Library Association (ALA). As a result, I joined the ALA during my final year of library school. After joining the ALA, I filled out committee volunteer forms seeking membership on ALA committees. Luckily, I was appointed to an ALA committee on my first attempt. Interestingly, while this was my first appointment to a professional committee, it is worth pointing out that I had already engaged in "public service" long before I became a librarian. In fact, I was a very active student in college. For example, I served as the president of the Vietnamese Student Association at my college. Later, at another university during my undergraduate years, I was elected vice president of the International Student Association. It is hard to imagine now that I was that engaged in college activities, given the fact that I was a penniless refugee who had set foot on American soil just a couple of years earlier.

Looking back at my public service history since then, I believe I possess a long, sustained, and distinguished public service record. At the college level, I have served on and chaired many of the library's and college's committees, including chairing the Penn State Abington College Faculty Senate. Penn State Abington College is one of the twentyfour campuses of the Pennsylvania State University, so this was a demanding responsibility. The chair of the Abington College Faculty Senate also serves as a member of the Chancellor's Cabinet and a member of the Faculty Advisory to the chancellor of the Abington College. The chancellor is the highest ranking administrator of the college. These are important positions in the administrative structure of the college. They are particularly important because the Penn State Abington College, as well as the Pennsylvania State University, is a sharedgovernance institution, which means that the faculty, through the University Faculty Senate (UFS), and the administration share the responsibility of governing the university. Over the past two decades, I have served on more than three dozen committees and have also chaired many of them. In 2007, in recognizing my exemplary public service contributions to the college, the Abington College Faculty Senate awarded me the Distinguished Faculty Service Award.

Besides serving on and leading many of the library's and college's committees, I was elected by the Abington College faculty to serve as a University Faculty Senator, representing the faculty of the Abington College to the University Faculty Senate of the Pennsylvania State University. I was also elected by the Abington College's University Faculty Senators to serve as a member of the University Faculty Senate Council of the Pennsylvania State University. The University Senate Council, an important leadership unit of the University Faculty Senate, is composed of councilors (University Faculty Senators who are elected by their fellow senators to represent them on the University Faculty Senate Council), senate leaders, and senior university administrators, including the provost and the president of the university. Since Penn State is a sharedgovernance institution, the University Faculty Senate plays a very important role in developing the university curriculum. In fact, its primary role is to oversee the university curriculum.

I have also been very active in professional organizations, including the Association of College and Research Libraries (ACRL), and so on. Over the years, I have served on and led many ACRL committees. For example, I was nominated and elected to serve as the chair of the Asian, African, and Middle Eastern Section of the ACRL twice. I have also served as chair of the following entities: ACRL/LPSS Marta Lange CQ/Press Award Committee (twice); ACRL/IRC; ACRL/AAMES (section chair, twice), ALA/IRC/East Asia and the Pacific Subcommittee; RUSA/Liaison with Users Committee; ACRL/AAMES Executive Committee; ACRL/AAMES Membership Committee; and so on. In recognition of my contributions to the library profession, I have received many honors, including the Marta Lange CQ Press Award, which recognizes "an academic or law librarian who, through research, service to the profession, or other creative activity, makes distinguished contributions to bibliography and information service in law or political science."[2] I have also served as a trustee of the Upper Moreland Public Library and as a member of the board of directors of the Library and Education Assistance Foundation for Vietnam (LEAFVN).

LITERATURE REVIEW

Public service is an important aspect of leadership development and attainment. Dorothy J. Anderson, in a study of the UCLA Senior Fellows Program, found that "senior fellows totaled more than twice as many professional activities as the ACRL matched group of 50, and nearly three times as many as the ACRL control group of 152."[3] The same study also found that the senior fellows are two or three times more active at the top levels of leadership.[4] My recent study on Asian American library leaders revealed that many Asian American library leaders have been very active in professional organizations.[5] One participant stated,

> I was very active at a point in my career, never missing an opportunity to serve in LLAMA, Council, etc. I served on a number of NISON and ISO committees on library statistics and measurement. I was active in IFLA, especially in the area of library statistics. Serving as the Director of the National Agricultural Library, I was very involved with national and international library organizations (USAIN, AgNIC), etc.[6]

Besides contributing to various organizations, public service has also been an important aspect of their leadership development. One participant stated,

> Holding leadership roles in professional organizations is one of the most important elements in the development of my library career. I was very active in ALA, ACRL, IFLA, ARL, etc., and held various key positions. The effect of networking with other library leaders at the state, national, and international levels was of great importance in my library career.[7]

It is also worthwhile to point out that many Asian American library leaders have also been very active at their colleges and universities as well. They served on library and college or university committees and task forces. One participant stated, "I was very active also in holding leadership positions in committees and task forces at several universities where I worked."[8] Interestingly, many of these leaders, as noted, have also been very active in international organizations. Like many of these Asian American library leaders, I have also found that public service has indeed played an important role in my leadership development and attainment.

Methodology

This section is a narrative of my leadership development and attainment. It focuses mainly on the public service activities in which I have participated throughout my professional career, both within and outside the academic world. My public service activities will be discussed under a "framework" that I have utilized in my other studies.[9] The principal aspects of this framework include the following elements: Engage in public service early; serve in the areas that one is familiar with; broaden public service areas (different areas of expertise, different organizational functions or types, etc.); assume leadership positions when offered; seek and attain leadership when opportunities present themselves; and seek employment at institutions that encourage, support, value, and reward public service.

Seek Committee Membership Early

After joining the ALA, I wasted no time in seeking out committee membership. Knowing that my understanding of ALA committee structure was limited, I deliberately chose committees that were less complex, less weighty, with limited charges and specific responsibilities. I also selected committees that had direct bearing on the job I held at the time and the areas that I had some basic knowledge of, for example, reference service and library instruction. Wisely, the ALA appointment committees assigned me to the committees that were suitable to my experience and interests. Similarly, some of my first committee assignments on campus included serving as a member on the college's Bookstore Committee as well as serving as a faculty advisor to the Asian Student Club. I was not interested in being a member of the standing committees of the College Faculty Senate, the Library Faculty Organization, and the University Faculty Senate because of my limited experience and knowledge in these areas. Despite not having an interest in serving on these committees, I followed them very closely because I knew that sooner or later I wanted to serve on them.

Expand Committee Membership

After a few years of serving on small and less complex committees, I understood how committees work and I had acquired a more indepth understanding about the committee structures of these organizations (e.g., my own college/university, ALA, ACRL). I gradually sought committee membership in larger, more complex, wideimpact, high visibility committees in these organizations. I also expanded my committee interests into more specialized areas, such as technology, management, leadership, and so on. As a result, I not only became a member of but also chaired many of the committees in the ACRL, RUSA, and LPSS.

Similarly, I also sought membership on the major or standing committees of the college, such as the Library Faculty Organization (LFO), which is an elective body representing the library faculty at Penn State whose duties include developing policies governing the library faculty, such as policies on promotion and tenure and faculty affairs. I nominated myself to be a senatorial candidate for the college's Faculty Senate. I also nominated myself for other elective positions in the LFO and the UFS. Luckily, I got elected to many of these positions. Once elected to these committees, I sought committee assignments that were suitable to my interests and experiences. In serving on these committees, I learned how these committees and organizations work. I also learned in greater depth many of the issues facing these organizations. In particular, I was interested in learning and observing how the leaders (chairs) of these committees exercise their leadership responsibilities, from managing basic protocols to dealing with complex issues.

I wanted to serve not only on a number of different committees but also on important committees. After being elected as a University Faculty Senator, I requested that the UFS leadership appoint me to important committees, such as the University Faculty Senate Committee on Curricular Affairs. Within the UFS structure, this committee is one of the most important. Its main responsibility is to oversee every aspect of the university curriculum, including graduation and degree requirements, courses, minors, majors, and so on. Every month, the committee reviews and approves a large number of curricular proposals, including courses, options, minors, and majors for the whole university. It is worthwhile to note that the Pennsylvania State University offers over 170 undergraduate degree programs as well as "more than 160 graduate majors or fields of study that include 92 research doctorates and eight professional doctoral fields."[10] The faculty, through the UFS, controls every aspect of the university curriculum.

Be Willing to Assume Leadership Positions

In the early stages of my career I did not seek leadership roles; however, I was propelled into leadership positions. I was asked or urged by members to take on the leadership roles of committees when the leadership of a committee was vacated either because a leader had resigned or his or her term had expired. Instead of declining these leadership opportunities, I accepted them. In fact, I became a leader of a number of committees this way. Interestingly, in some cases, because of a lack of experience or expertise, I agreed to chair a committee, especially a large or complex one, only if another member was willing to cochair that committee with me. In asking another member to cochair a committee, I usually asked for an experienced and respected member. My objectives were to search for capable people who would not only help me accomplish the tasks we were charged with, but who would also help my leadership development as well.

In chairing and cochairing small and less complex committees, I gained a considerable amount of leadership experience. I also gained a lot of confidence in my leadership ability. In addition, in serving in these leadership roles, I started to know more people, including senior leaders of the organizations. These factors have made me feel comfortable in seeking out greater leadership roles and responsibilities. After several years of serving in these capacities, I was, in fact, ready to seek greater leadership roles on larger and more complex committees. Thus, whenever a committee leadership position was open, I openly expressed my willingness to serve by telling the people or entities responsible for appointing leaders to those committees about my desire to chair those committees. Unlike in the past when I waited for people to approach me for leadership positions, I now actively sought out leadership roles. I carefully examined the bylaws of these organizations concerning their leadership selection process and followed them carefully. For example, if an elective leadership position required nomination by colleagues or nominating committees, I sought appropriate nominations. If a leadership position required selfnomination, I nominated myself. Luckily, over the years, I have seldom failed to attain the leadership positions I sought.

In order to advance to higher leadership positions, one must possess a record of leadership accomplishments. In addition to successfully accomplishing the tasks that the committees are charged with, good committee leaders achieve much more. For example, when I chaired the AAMES I not only organized the annual conference program but also initiated the AAMES Annual Research Colloquium. The program has been a success. In fact, it has been AAMES's annual program since. Similarly, when I chaired the ALA/IRC/East Asia and the Pacific Subcommittee (2014–15), I also initiated, organized, and moderated the ALA/IRC/EAP Subcommittee Research Forum at the 2015 ALA annual meeting. It proved to be another successful program. The program included speakers from outside the United States. The members of this subcommittee have already decided that there will be a research forum during the 2016 ALA annual meeting in Orlando. At the college level, for example, when serving as cochair of the college's Academic Environment Committee, I proposed that the college should celebrate the scholarly and artistic accomplishments of the college's faculty. After the committee accepted this proposal, I organized the college's first "FacultyAuthor" event.[11] It was a great success and has been a major annual event for more than a decade.

Seek Institutional Support

Public service contributes to the organization's goals and purposes as well as the individual's personal, professional, and leadership development. But public service takes a considerable amount of an individual's and institution's resources and commitment. Consequently, one must choose carefully the institutions where one works. It is best to work for institutions that not only encourage, reward, and value public service, but also provide the resources needed for one to participate in public service at the state, national, and international levels.

The fact is that one cannot participate in professional activities without being a member of professional organizations. The problem, however, is that membership fees of professional organizations are expensive. In addition, members of committees and especially committee leaders are required to attend professional conferences. For example, if one is a member of an ALA committee, he or she must agree to attend both its annual and its midwinter conferences. However, the costs (e.g., registration, lodging, meals, and transportation) of attending professional conferences, especially national and international conferences, are high. For example, the typical registration fee for an IFLA conference is above $600. Furthermore, IFLA annual conferences, like those of its ALA counterpart, are often held in large and expensive cities, such as Seoul or Helsinki. It is even more challenging for subject librarians (e.g., area studies librarians, music librarians, arts librarians) who, in addition to being members of the ALA, may also have to belong to specialized organizations (e.g., the Association for Asian Studies), which hold their own annual conferences. In fact, it is virtually impossible for many librarians to attend these conferences if no institutional support is available. Furthermore, institutions must also grant release time for participation in public service because public service requires one to invest a considerable amount of time. Besides providing financial support and release time for public service, institutions must also reward those who provide exemplary public service, particularly those who demonstrate exemplary or successful leadership achievements in the service area at their own institutions and at the state, national, and international levels. At Penn State, public service is one of the three major elements (teaching/librarianship, research, and service) of the promotion and tenure process.

I have been fortunate enough to work for an institution that expects me to actively engage in public service at all levels. Penn State also rewards my service contributions to the University Libraries and the university itself, as well as state, national, and international library and educational organizations. Besides my accomplishments in librarianship and research, the university particularly rewards my contributions in the public service area, particularly the leadership accomplishments I have achieved in various organizations.

CONCLUSION

To serve or not to serve is the question. For me, the answer to this question is obvious. For more than two decades, I have made significant public service contributions to my college and university; to the local, state, national, and international library organizations; to higher education institutions at home and abroad; and to nonprofit organizations. But serving these entities it has also benefited me enormously. In particular, seeking, holding, and succeeding at leadership positions through public service have significantly contributed to my leadership development and attainment (communication skills, organizational skills, teamwork, etc.). I have also had opportunities to work with some of the most influential, talented, and dedicated leaders in the library field and in higher education worldwide. Above all, it has helped in cultivating me to be not just an effective leader but also a better human being.

Notes

1. Penn State University, Administrative Fellows Program webpage, Office of the Vice Provost for Academic Affairs accessed August 20, 2015 http://www.psu.edu/dept/vprov/adminfellows.htm.
2. Association of College and Research Libraries, "Marta Lange/SAGECQ Press Award," accessed September 9, 2015 http://www.ala.org/acrl/awards/achievementawards/martalangecq.
3. Dorothy J. Anderson, "Comparative Career Profiles of Academic Librarians: Are Leaders Different?" *Journal of Academic Librarianship* 10, no. 6 (January 1985): 326.
4. Ibid., 330.
5. Binh P. Le, "Asian Americans and American Academic Libraries: Pathways to Leadership" (Ed.D. diss., Wilmington University, 2013).
6. Ibid., 74.
7. Ibid., 75–76.
8. Ibid., 75.
9. Le, "Asian Americans," and Binh P. Le, "Attainment of Academic Library Leadership by Asian Americans: Challenges and Development," in *Creating Sustainable Community*, ed. Dawn M. Mueller (Chicago: Association of College and Research Libraries, 2015), 28–39.
10. "Graduate School Dean Follows Circuitous Path to Senior Leadership," Penn State News, August 10, 2015, last updated August 11, 2015, http://news.psu.edu/story/365332/2015/08/10/academics/graduate-school-dean-follows-circuitous-path-senior-leadership.
11. John Riddle, Binh Le, and Rebecca Mugridge, "The Value of Faculty Recognition Programs for Libraries: More Than Just 'Good Will'," *Library Administration and Management* 19 (2005): 75–81.

Bibliography

Anderson, Dorothy J. "Comparative Career Profiles of Academic Librarians: Are Leaders Different?" *Journal of Academic Librarianship* 10, no. 6 (January 1985): 326–32.

Association of College and Research Libraries. "Marta Lange/SAGECQ Press Award," Accessed September 9, 2015, http://www.ala.org/acrl/awards/ achievementawards/martalangecq.

Committee on Institutional Cooperation webpage. Office of the Vice Provost for Academic Affairs. Accessed August 20, 2015, http://www.psu.edu/dept/vprov/ cic.htm.

Le, Binh P. "Asian Americans and American Academic Libraries: Pathways to Leadership." Ed.D. diss., Wilmington University, 2013.

————."Attainment of Academic Library Leadership by Asian Americans: Challenges and Development," In *Creating Sustainable Community: ACRL 2015 Proceedings,* Edited by Dawn M. Mueller, 28–39. Chicago: Association of College and Research Libraries, 2015. http://www.ala.org/acrl/sites/ala.org.acrl/files/ content/conferences/confsandpreconfs/2015/Le.pdf.

Penn State News, "Graduate School Dean Follows Circuitous Path to Senior Leadership," August 10, 2015, last updated August 11, 2015, http://news.psu .edu/story/365332/2015/08/10/academics/graduate-school-dean-follows -circuitous-path-senior-leadership. Penn State University. Administrative Fellows Program webpage. Office of the Vice Provost for Academic Affairs, Accessed August 20, 2015, http://www.psu.edu/dept/vprov/adminfellows.htm.

Riddle, John, Binh Le, and Rebecca Mugridge, "The Value of Faculty Recognition Programs for Libraries: More Than Just 'Good Will'," *Library Administration and Management* 19 (2005): 75–81.

Chapter 10

CONCLUSION

Antonia P. Olivas

STUDIES SHOW THAT a lack of diversity leads to several issues, such as a biased selection of research, uniformity of opinion, poor decision making, and a mistrust.[1] Although the American Library Association is committed to recruiting more underrepresented minority librarians, numbers still show that white females continue to dominate the profession.[2] There is a widely held opinion that the profession is not doing enough to properly retain and promote underrepresented minority librarians in the profession. Many academic librarians express a sense of frustration with the lack of opportunity provided to librarians of color currently in the field. We hear stories of underrepresented minority librarians feeling like they are being boxed into "diversity" positions and not offered other leadership roles. As a result, many of these librarians feel they have to seek leadership positions outside their libraries in order to receive the experience they need to succeed. Finally, some librarians of color experience feelings of isolation and therefore seek diverse professional relationships through ALA-sponsored caucuses such as REFORMA, AILA and BCALA.

Right now academic libraries are most often led by white women and men, yet we are told that the racial makeup of students attending colleges and universities is changing. As more diverse student populations graduate from high school and seek postsecondary opportunities, the numbers of underrepresented minority educators, namely librarians, will need to keep up in order to help these students succeed.[3]

Library leaders help students succeed through developing library services, collecting diverse resources, and creating a welcoming environment for all students, most especially underrepresented minority students.[4]

We know there are underrepresented minority academic librarians willing to lead; the chapters within this book tell their stories. Unfortunately there still aren't enough to meet the radically changing needs of our diverse student populations attending our colleges and universities. The essays in this book helped to shed some light on some of the motivational factors behind people of color taking on leadership roles at their institutions. We read personal accounts of how they overcame difficulties in the profession and what dynamic and creative ways they sought positions of leadership, be it formal or informal. Many of the authors expressed feelings of obligation to their communities, their families, and the profession for taking on these roles. Others admitted to actively seeking leadership opportunities, both in and out of libraries, based on the sheer joy of leading others.

It is safe to say that there is no one definition of leadership, and that all of the authors in this book display one form or another of library leadership qualities. Their chapters delved into what motivates them to continue on their paths and touched on what aspiring underrepresented minority academic library leaders can do to help accomplish their goals. We have read the literature that talks about the barriers librarians of color face in the profession, but it is also important to learn from the success stories to help increase the retention and promotion numbers of underrepresented minority academic library leaders.

This book asked authors to delve into their own motivations to lead to explore the reasons that help them stay in the library profession and pursue leadership positions within the field. Allowing authors to share their own leadership stories in their own words allowed for a more inclusive look at their motivations to lead and provided a better understanding of the issues they faced by focusing on the more comprehensive details of their lived experiences. Using an appreciative inquiry approach to help elicit in-depth stories, the authors provided more insight into what motivates them to stay in the profession and seek leadership opportunities.

Motivation to Lead Theory in Action

Most leadership research focuses on personality traits, but MTL goes beyond personality. Motivation to Lead theory does not assume people are born to lead or that people have an unconscious desire for power;[5] instead MTL assumes that leadership skills, leadership style, and the understanding of what it means to be a leader are learned over time.[6] A major hypothesis of MTL theory is that personality traits in addition to individual values, behaviors, self-efficacy, and past leadership experience affect a person's motivation to want to lead.

As mentioned in the introduction, MTL theory measures three correlated factors: *Affective Identity, Non-calculative Identity,* and *Social-Normative Identity.* How were these identities manifested throughout the book? As a refresher, here are brief definitions of each identity:

- Affective identity suggests that leaders like leading for the pure enjoyment of leading others.

- Non-calculative identity says that leaders do not consider the cost when seeking leadership positions.

- Social-Normative identity leaders feel a sense of obligation, a strong sense of duty to lead.

Factors That Influence Motivation to Lead

There were several factors that authors in this book credited with staying in the profession. Some of those included things like having a strong sense of passion for some aspect of librarianship, having a certain amount of self-confidence and persistence when faced with obstacles, pairing up with respected mentors, and networking with other underrepresented academic librarians. In addition to these reasons, the authors' chapters highlighted two major themes woven throughout. Those themes included a sense of obligation (either to the self or to others) and a sense of contentment or reward for a job well done.

Sense of obligation. Research has shown that employees driven by a sense of obligation, rather than personal ambition, are more likely to work toward the benefit of their greater organization and speak up more at work.[7] When one thinks of the word *obligation*, usually negative con-notations arise—where a person feels bound to do something based on guilt or to repay a debt. The term *obligation*, in the context of MTL, how-ever, does not necessarily reflect something negative, especially for these authors. On the contrary, most of the authors expressed a strong sense of honor and pride when they talked about their obligations to family and to their communities. Most of the authors in this book felt like they had to lead based on a sense of obligation and responsibility, usually to them-selves but sometimes to others. Some of the authors clearly stated they wanted to take leadership positions because they felt no one else would or could perform the job to their own high standards. All of these librarians take pride in their work and want to ensure their organizations are doing all they could to help support student learning needs. The authors in the book have a strong desire to succeed in meeting challenges placed before them and often found themselves taking on roles that no one else wanted to or could take.

There were also feelings of obligation based on the fact that most of these authors were "one of a kind" in their libraries and no one else from their ethnic backgrounds could represent those important voices if they left. McElroy-Johnson stated that "Voice is power...."[8] For the authors in this book and many underrepresented minority librarians in the profes-sion, voice represents participation in an elite organization where they bring others to the table. Several of the authors cautioned that they are not speaking for every minority person at their university, but they also felt that other "majority member" librarians may not fully understand the "voiceless" and may not be able to accurately represent those particular needs. In addition to wanting to give voice to others, some of the authors wanted to "give back" to others who have gone before them, and others wanted to "pay it forward" to a new set of diverse librarians who will even-tually follow in their own footsteps.

Several of the authors credited family obligation as one of the main reasons for staying in the profession. Studies have shown that individu-als from underrepresented minority backgrounds exhibit high degrees of loyalty and commitment to their families.[9] One of the ways some of the authors in this book demonstrate respect for their families is to succeed in their current professions. Therefore, family respect and responsibility strongly motivated their desires to stay and lead.

Feelings of contentment. Beyond potential monetary returns, the authors in this book expressed feelings of joy or contentment because of their simple desire to lead. This means that the authors who shared more of these feelings showed they valued *Non-calculative* and *Affective* identities more. This means that authors did look at the benefits and rewards when taking leadership positions, but they seemed to look at those rewards based on feelings of pleasure in leading. As stated before, many of the authors weighed the needs of their communities, their libraries, and their families before deciding to take leadership roles. Interestingly, Sorkhabi conducted a study on interpersonal relationships and found that participants calculated the costs and consequences to both themselves and those they were contemplating helping.[10] The author found that participants' sense of moral obligations to help was greater when both the recipient and the participant faced higher levels of need. That explains why these authors talked about their sense of reward and the positive feelings associated with doing a good job and helping others. Many of the authors in this book said (or implied) that they genuinely enjoyed seeking and participating in leadership positions.

Understanding MTL's Role in Retention and Promotion

This book encourages current academic library leaders to dig deeper and instead of focusing on personalities, recognize the multidimensional nature of their underrepresented minority librarians and examine what keeps them in the profession. Give librarians autonomy, encourage them to better their skills, and give them a purpose to do something meaningful.[11] We challenge current library leaders to learn to use MTL to recognize their librarians' individual differences, which are closely related to their librarians' interests and abilities. As time goes on, librarians' individual motivations to lead can change with leadership experiences and training, so current library leaders must learn to recognize those changes and be flexible to encourage growth in their librarians. Getting to know minority librarian passions and current motivations will help current library leaders establish a leadership development plan and create a positive work environment. Ultimately this will help the career trajectory of underrepresented minority librarians and could potentially lead to a more diverse workforce in academic library leadership. In order to accomplish this, current library leaders must be willing to think outside the box, beyond diversity recruitment efforts and beyond simply mentoring.

Understanding the role of employee motivation is an important tool that all leaders need to learn how to use. However, understanding motivation in academic libraries, specifically the motivation to lead of underrepresented minority librarians, is often completely overlooked by today's library leaders. Current library leaders can use their understanding of Motivation to Lead theory to help inspire more underrepresented minority librarians to take on leadership roles. Not all motivation comes from the outside; each individual has his or her own set of motivating factors that are more intrinsic. It is the responsibility of current library leaders to carefully identify and address these motivating factors and build strategic leadership development plans for each of their librarians. Current library leaders must create positive work environments and provide leadership opportunities for all of their librarians. Although there are many individual factors that contribute to a librarian's motivation to lead, current library leaders must work with their librarians to identify, on individual levels, successful processes and programs that will work for their career goals. Take the time to get to know the librarians of color in the organization and their career personal career trajectories before tasking them with projects that may not fit their purpose.

Identifying individual motivational factors may sound tedious and time-consuming, but it is less costly than constant librarian turnover. People tend to want to stay in a place where they feel valued and appreciated for a job well done. A library leader who takes the time to find out that the African American social sciences librarian she just hired a few months ago also has a passion for social justice and equity issues may task him with taking the lead on developing projects and programs for the library. That could eventually lead to larger leadership roles of tasking him to work with campus committees to help develop campus-wide programs and policies. Each step in the individual's leadership development plan should be carefully planned and considered as an ongoing discussion between the current library leader and the academic librarian of color.

Once a leadership development plan, based on the academic librarian's passions and motivations, is clearly identified, it is important the library leader recognize and reward her librarians accordingly. As stated before, motivation is both intrinsic and extrinsic. Academic library leaders should not assume that all people feel valued and appreciated just because they continue to be productive. Current library leaders should also not assume that the recognition and reward system that works for one librarian will work for others. Although no one in this book mentioned that monetary incentives were a motivational factor for these authors, it does not suggest people do not want to be compensated for the good work they do. Incentives can be both monetary and nonmonetary. The current budgetary landscape for academic libraries does not always allow for pay increases or financial compensation, but a library leader should be on the lookout for professional development opportunities that are free or reasonable in pricing to include their underrepresented minority academic librarians. Again, the reward is based on the librarian's comfort and preference.[12]

POTENTIAL FOR FUTURE RESEARCH

Much of the current research on leadership looks at leader characteristics and how those influence organizational success. Literature on diversity in academic libraries generally focuses on why underrepresented minority librarians leave the profession. To date, there is very little research that investigates the reasons librarians of color stay, much less investigates their individual motivations to lead. In order to understand retention and promotion of underrepresented minority academic librarians, it is important to understand the obstacles these librarians face and what motivates them to pursue leadership positions in a predominantly white profession. Further quantitative and qualitative research on the motivation to lead of underrepresented minority librarians is needed. To date, very little research looks at motivation to lead in librarianship.[13] Research using Motivation to Lead theory focusing mainly on current underrepresented minority library leaders could help establish a baseline for future research on potential library leaders. More research on retention efforts and motivational factors can present practical implications for leadership selection, training, and development in university libraries. In researching library leaders' motivations to lead, one could discover additional motivational factors that will help expand the range of motivational factors beyond what is discussed in this study.[14]

Simply looking at the failing retention and promotion efforts that affect minority librarians limits the body of knowledge available to help investigate what does work to increase these numbers. While a majority of the current library research focuses on diversity recruitment efforts, with the exception of a handful of ARL retention programs, there is little research on successful retention and promotion strategies that universities themselves can put in place. Not all universities are associated with ARL; therefore, those libraries also need effective programs to help retain current minority librarians and develop potential library leaders.

NOTES

1. Yoel Inbar and Joris Lammers, "Political Diversity in Social and Personality Psychology," *Perspectives on Psychological Science* 7, no. 5 (September 2012): 496–503, doi:10.1177/1745691612448792; Dennis M. Kivlighan, "Compositional Diversity and the Research Productivity of PhD Graduates," *Journal of Diversity in Higher Education* 1, no. 1 (March 2008): 59–66.
2. American Library Association, "ALA Demographic Studies," March 2012, http://www.ala.org/research/sites/ala.org.research/files/content/March%202012%20report.pdf.
3. Thomas D. Snyder and Sally A. Dillow, "Table 287: Employees in Degree-Granting Institutions, by Race/Ethnicity, Sex, Employment Status, Control and Level of Institution, and Primary Occupation: Fall 2011," *Digest of Education Statistics, 2012*, NCES 2014015 (Washington, DC: National Center for Education Statistics, December 2013), 415, https://nces.ed.gov/programs/digest/d12/tables/dt12_287.asp.
4. Tracie D. Hall, "Race and Place: How Unequal Access Perpetuates Exclusion," *American Libraries* 38, no. 2 (February 2007): 30–33.
5. Thomas Carlyle, *On Heroes, Hero-Worship, and the Heroic in History* (Ann Arbor: University of Michigan Library, 2005), first published 1859, http://name.umdl.umich.edu/ABE9468.0001.001; David C. McClelland, *Power* (Cambridge: Cambridge University Press, 1985); David C. McClelland, *Human Motivation* (New York: Irvington, 1975); John B. Miner, *Motivation to Manage* (Atlanta, GA: Organizational Measurement Systems Press. 1977); John B. Miner, *Role Motivation Theories* (London: Routledge, 1993); Michael J. Stahl, *Managerial and Technical Motivation* (New York: Westport, 1986).
6. Kim-Yin Chan, "Toward a Theory of Individual Differences and Leadership: Understanding the Motivation to Lead" (PhD diss., University of Illinois at Urbana-Champaign, 1999), http://hdl.handle.net/2142/82262; Kim-Yin Chan and Fritz Drasgow, "Toward a Theory of Individual Differences and Leadership: Understanding the Motivation to Lead," *Journal of Applied Psychology* 86, no. 3 (June 2001): 481–95, https://www.researchgate.net/publication/11920242_Toward _a_Theory_of_Individual_Differences_and_Leadership.

7. Subrahmaniam Tangirala, Dishan Kamdar, Vijaya Venkataramani, and Michael R. Parke, "Doing Right versus Getting Ahead: The Effects of Duty and Achievement Orientations on Employees' Voice," *Journal of Applied Psychology* 98, no. 6 (November 2013): 1040–50, EBSCOhost PsycARTICLES, http://dx.doi.org.ezproxy .csusm.edu/10.1037/a0033855.

8. Beverly McElroy-Johnson, "Giving Voice to the Voiceless," *Harvard Educational Review* 63, no. 1 (1993): 86, ERIC, 62871067.

9. Marilyn Coleman, Lawrence Ganong, and Tanja Rothrauff, "Acculturation and Latinos' Beliefs about Intergenerational Obligations to Older Parents and Stepparents," *Journal of Intergenerational Relationships* 5, no. 3 (2007): 65–82, EBSCOhost Academic Search Premier, http://dx.doi.org/10.1300/J194v05n03_05; Karen L. Fingerman, Laura E. VanderDrift, Aryn M. DottereZaritr, Kira S. Birditt, and Steven H. Zarit, "Support to Aging Parents and Grown Children in Black and White Families," *Gerontologist* 51, no. 4 (August 2011): 441–52, EBSCOhost Academic Search Premier, doi:10.1093/geront/gnq114; Andrew J. Fuligni, "Family Obligation and the Academic Motivation of Adolescents from Asian and Latin American, and European Backgrounds," in *Family Obligation and Assistance during Adolescence: Contextual Variations and Developmental Implications,* ed. Andrew J. Fuligni (San Francisco: Jossey-Bass, 2001), 61–76; Andrew J. Fuligni, Vivian Tseng, and May Lam, "Attitudes toward Family Obligations among American Adolescents with Asian, Latin American, and European Backgrounds," *Child Development* 70, no. 4 (July 1999): 1030–45, EBSCOhost Academic Search Premier, doi: 10.1111/1467–8624.00075; Lisa Groger and Pamela Mayberry, "Caring Too Much? Cultural Lag in African Americans' Perceptions of Filial Responsibilities," *Journal of Cross-Cultural Gerontology* 16, no. 1 (March 2001): 21–40, EBSCOhost Academic Search Premier, doi: 10.1023/A:1010637510362.

10. Nadia Sorkhabi, "Care Reasoning in Interpersonal Relationships: Cognition about Moral Obligation and Personal Choice," *North American Journal of Psychology* 14, no. 2 (June 2012): 221–44, ProQuest ABI/INFORM Complete New Platform (ECC Resource), 1013609994.

11. Daniel H. Pink, *Drive* (New York: Riverhead Books, 2011).

12. Ian Bessell, Brad Dicks, Allen Wysocki, Karl Kepner, Derek Farnsworth, and Jennifer L. Clark, "Understanding Motivation: An Effective Tool for Managers," University of Florida IFAS Extension, originally published June 2002, revised October 2015, http://edis.ifas.ufl.edu/hr017.

13. Antonia P. Olivas, "Understanding Underrepresented Minority Academic Librarian's Motivation to Lead in Higher Education" (PhD diss., University of California, San Diego, California State University, San Marcos, 2014).

14. Karin Amit, Alon Lisak, Micha Popper, and Reuven Gal, "Motivation to Lead: Research on the Motives for Undertaking Leadership Roles in the Israel Defense Forces," *Military Psychology* 19, no. 3 (2007): 137–60; Chan, "Toward a Theory of Individual Differences"; Chan and Drasgow, "Toward a Theory of Individual Differences."

BIBLIOGRAPHY

American Library Association. "ALA Demographic Studies." March 2012. http://www
.ala.org/research/sites/ala.org.research/files/content/March%202012%20
report.pdf.

Amit, Karin, Alon Lisak, Micha Popper, and Reuven Gal. "Motivation to Lead: Research on the Motives for Undertaking Leadership Roles in the Israel Defense
Forces." *Military Psychology* 19, no. 3 (2007): 137–60.

Bessell, Ian, Brad Dicks, Allen Wysocki, Karl Kepner, Derek Farnsworth, and Jennifer
L. Clark. "Understanding Motivation: An Effective Tool for Managers." University of Florida IFAS Extension. Originally published June 2002, revised October
2015. http://edis.ifas.ufl.edu/hr017.

Carlyle, Thomas. *On Heroes, Hero-Worship, and the Heroic in History*. Ann Arbor:
University of Michigan Library, 2005. First published 1859. http://name.umdl
.umich.edu/ABE9468.0001.001.

Chan, Kim-Yin. "Toward a Theory of Individual Differences and Leadership: Understanding the Motivation to Lead." PhD diss., University of Illinois at Urbana-Champaign, 1999. http://hdl.handle.net/2142/82262.

Chan, Kim-Yin, and Fritz Drasgow. "Toward a Theory of Individual Differences and
Leadership: Understanding the Motivation to Lead." *Journal of Applied Psychology* 86, no. 3 (June 2001): 481–95. https://www.researchgate.net/publication/
11920242_Toward_a_Theory_of_Individual_Differences_and_Leadership.

Coleman, Marilyn, Lawrence Ganong, and Tanja Rothrauff. "Acculturation and Latinos' Beliefs about Intergenerational Obligations to Older Parents and Stepparents." *Journal of Intergenerational Relationships* 5, no. 3 (2007): 65–82. EBSCO-
host Academic Search Premier, doi: http://dx.doi.org/10.1300/J194v05n03
_05.

Fingerman, Karen L., Laura E. VanderDrift, Aryn M. DottereZaritr, Kira S. Birditt, and
Steven H. Zarit. "Support to Aging Parents and Grown Children in Black and
White Families." *Gerontologist* 51, no. 4 (August 2011): 441–52. EBSCOhost
Academic Search Premier, doi:10.1093/geront/gnq114.

Fuligni, Andrew J. "Family Obligation and the Academic Motivation of Adolescents
from Asian and Latin American, and European Backgrounds." In *Family Obligation and Assistance during Adolescence: Contextual Variations and Developmental
Implications*. Edited by Andrew J. Fuligni, 61–76. San Francisco: Jossey-Bass,
2001.

Fuligni, Andrew J., Vivian Tseng, and May Lam. "Attitudes toward Family Obligations
among American Adolescents with Asian, Latin American, and European
Backgrounds." *Child Development* 70, no. 4 (July 1999): 1030–45. EBSCOhost
Academic Search Premier, doi: 10.1111/1467–8624.00075.

Groger, Lisa, and Pamela Mayberry. "Caring Too Much? Cultural Lag in African Americans' Perceptions of Filial Responsibilities." *Journal of Cross-Cultural Gerontology* 16, no. 1 (March 2001): 21–40. EBSCOhost Academic Search Premier, doi:
10.1023/A:1010637510362.

Hall, Tracie D. "Race and Place: How Unequal Access Perpetuates Exclusion." *American Libraries* 38, no. 2 (February 2007): 30–33.

Inbar, Yoel, and Joris Lammers. "Political Diversity in Social and Personality Psychology." *Perspectives on Psychological Science* 7, no. 5 (September 2012): 496–503. doi:10.1177/1745691612448792.

Kivlighan, Dennis M. "Compositional Diversity and the Research Productivity of PhD Graduates." *Journal of Diversity in Higher Education* 1, no. 1 (March 2008): 59–66.

McClelland, David C. *Human Motivation*. Cambridge: Cambridge University Press, 1985.

———. *Power: The Inner Experience*. New York: Irvington, 1975.

McElroy-Johnson, Beverly. "Giving Voice to the Voiceless." *Harvard Educational Review* 63, no. 1 (1993): 85–104. ERIC, 62871067.

Miner, John, B. *Motivation to Manage: A Ten Year Update on the Studies in Management Education Research*. Atlanta, GA: Organizational Measurement Systems Press. 1977.

Miner, John, B. *Role Motivation Theories*. London: Routledge, 1993.

Olivas, Antonia P. "Understanding Underrepresented Minority Academic Librarian's Motivation to Lead in Higher Education." PhD diss., University of California, San Diego, California State University, San Marcos, 2014.

Pink, Daniel H. *Drive: The Surprising Truth about What Motivates Us*. New York: Riverhead Books, 2011.

Snyder, Thomas D., and Sally A. Dillow. "Table 287: Employees in Degree-Granting Institutions, by Race/Ethnicity, Sex, Employment Status, Control and Level of Institution, and Primary Occupation: Fall 2011." *Digest of Education Statistics, 2012*, NCES 2014015, 415. Washington, DC: National Center for Education Statistics, December 2013. https://nces.ed.gov/programs/digest/d12/tables/dt12_287.asp.

Sorkhabi, Nadia. "Care Reasoning in Interpersonal Relationships: Cognition about Moral Obligation and Personal Choice." *North American Journal of Psychology* 14, no. 2 (June 2012): 221–44. ProQuest ABI/INFORM Complete New Platform (ECC Resource), 1013609994.

Stahl, Michael, J. *Managerial and Technical Motivation: Assessing Needs for Achievement, Power and Affiliation*. New York: Westport, 1986.

Tangirala, Subrahmaniam, Dishan Kamdar, Vijaya Venkataramani, and Michael R. Parke. "Doing Right versus Getting Ahead: The Effects of Duty and Achievement Orientations on Employees' Voice." *Journal of Applied Psychology* 98, no. 6 (November 2013): 1040–50. EBSCOhost PsycARTICLES, doi: http://dx.doi.org.ezproxy.csusm.edu/10.1037/a0033855.